transforming together

transforming together

Authentic Spiritual Mentoring

ele parrott

MOODY PUBLISHERS

CHICAGO

All Scripture quotations, unless otherwise indicated, are taken from the *Holy Bible, New International Version®*. NIV®. Copyright © 1973, 1978, 1984 by International Bible Society. Used by permission of Zondervan. All rights reserved.

Scripture quotations marked NLT are taken from the *Holy Bible, New Living Translation*, copyright © 1996, 2004. Used by permission of Tyndale House Publishers, Inc., Wheaton, Illinois 60189, U.S.A. All rights reserved.

All websites and phone numbers listed herein are accurate at the time of publication, but may change in the future or cease to exist. The listing of website references and resources does not imply publisher endorsement of the site's entire contents. Groups and organizations are listed for informational purposes, and listing does not imply publisher endorsement of their activities.

Editor: Dana Wilkerson
Interior Design: Ragont Design
Cover Design: John Hamilton Design
Cover Image: iStockPhoto

Library of Congress Cataloging-in-Publication Data

Parrott, Ele.
    Transforming together : authentic spiritual mentoring / Ele Parrott.
      p. cm.
    ISBN 978-0-8024-6661-7
    1. Christian women—Religious life. 2. Mentoring in church work.
  3. Women in church work. I. Title.

BV4527.P35 2009
253.082—dc22

2008049486

We hope you enjoy this book from Moody Publishers. Our goal is to provide high quality, thought-provoking books and products that connect truth to your real needs and challenges. For more information on other books and products written and produced from a biblical perspective, go to www.moodypublishers.com or write to:

Moody Publishers
820 N. LaSalle Boulevard
Chicago, IL 60610

1 3 5 7 9 10 8 6 4 2

Printed in the United States of America

*It is with much joy that I dedicate this book
to each amazing woman that the Lord has brought into my life.
You know who you are.
I am overwhelmed that this earthly journey has been
constantly enriched by the investment of life on life with you,
by hearing your hearts, and by watching in amazement
as you grow more and more like your Savior, Jesus.*

*I also dedicate this book
to all of you who desire such a mentor/mentee relationship.
You know who you are as well!
My prayer is that the Lord will grant you the desire of your heart.
Be prayerful; be seeking one another with the eyes of grace and truth.
You will certainly find one another
and thus begin your journey of transforming together.*

Contents

Acknowledgments

As stated in the introduction, "this book has been grown" over many years. As iron sharpens iron so has my husband, Don, been used of the Lord to sharpen me over the past thirty-five-plus years. I so appreciate you, Don, and thank the Lord daily for allowing us to "accomplish together what He has for us"! May it continue to be so.

I also would like to acknowledge the editor of this book, Dana. What a quick but fun ride we have shared! It has been pure joy to work with you. I appreciate your eye, your words, your heart.

Also, I am very grateful for the group of prayer warriors who have carried this project from inception to completion. Our Father, who sees in secret, knows who you are. Great is your reward in heaven.

Finally, I want to express my gratitude to the women whose lives are represented in this book. You are light in a dark world. You are salt, enhancing and preserving truth in your lives. May your tribe increase!

Introduction

I've lived all my life to write this book.

Some books are birthed. This one was grown. The lessons of life come as a result of time: a result of experience, of choices, of living life directed by the Holy Spirit. The contents of this book are a direct result of just that—living life with Jesus. A spiritual mentor is also grown. Spiritual mentors are formed by living on this earth and experiencing all the "stuff" that life throws at them, but mentors are also focused on being led through it all by the Holy Spirit for God's glory and their good. One who desires to be a spiritual mentor is seasoned by occurrences, by happenings, by choices, by decisions—the ebb and flow of life with the Holy Spirit, who infuses His truth into our reality. There are no shortcuts to being a mentor. It's an honor that comes by living, by aging, and by becoming more like Jesus.

Like I said, "I've lived all my life to write this book."

When I was in my twenties, overwhelmed by four small children and a very full life, I often wondered, "Where are the older women? Doesn't anyone see I'm drowning here?" Or worse, "Doesn't anyone care that I'm going under for the third time?" I felt like I was constantly shoring myself up and limping through moments of self-doubt, self-hate, loneliness, and a lack of self-worth. Looking from the outside, very few others saw the pain, the ache, and the resentment that were growing in the pit of my being. After all, I was a pastor's wife. I was a leader in the women's ministry of our large church, I worked in the kids' ministries, and I ran a small cottage business on the side. My home was clean and in order. My children were dressed, their hair was combed, and they were well fed (if gummy bears and Goldfish crackers count). I led a small Bible study for women, filled in all the blanks every week, answered each question correctly (well, almost), sang in the church choir, and played the piano to boot! Pretty impressive, isn't it?

However, in the core of my being—in the depth of my soul—I knew there was more . . . or I *hoped* there was more, for, if this was all there was to being a follower of Jesus, I was sorely disappointed, angry, and scared. There *had* to be more—more spiritual insight, more emotional energy, more purpose of living, and a deeper source from which to draw forth love, kindness, caring, and interest for others. I knew that in Titus 2:4–5 we were told that the older women "can train the younger women to love their husbands and children, to be self-controlled and pure, to be busy at home, to be kind." I knew what it said, but I desperately desired to feel the results of such a relationship in my own life. And so I vowed that when I was an older woman I would purpose to be there for younger women.

Like I said, "I've lived all my life to write this book." And with good reason, because after being married to the same man for thirty-five years, raising those four children, living in five different countries, and now having grandchildren, I have had countless life experiences through which the Lord has dealt with me, grown me up, and made me a bit more like Himself. And that lifetime of experiences can be useful to others. I am now one of the "older women" mentioned in Titus 2. God has been incredibly persistent and faithful to me over the years. He has mentored me. He has helped to mature me, and He continues to do so even as I type these words. His Spirit, through His Word, has counseled me, taught me, corrected me, cautioned me, disciplined me, encouraged me, enlightened me, and comforted me. I am incredibly thankful to Him for His hand of mentorship on my life.

My prayer is that the thoughts, ideas, and teachings in this book will be of help to you. I hope that you will be able to identify with what is written; that it will encourage you, challenge you, and help you whether you are a spiritual mentor or someone who wants to be mentored. You will notice that the book is written from both perspectives: being a spiritual mentor and being a mentee. The spiritual mentors are written for us older gals who desire to be effective in the lives of younger women. Other chapters of the book are about younger women who are being mentored—their stories, their perspectives, and how Jesus is mentoring them through an older woman. May the Holy Spirit—our mentor—teach you, encourage you, and cause you to become more like Him as you read this book.

Just so you know, the stories of the younger women are composites. They were put together just for this book. The events are true, but the names, locations, and details are packaged in a way that will protect the privacy of these incredible women. I trust that you will be able to relate to them . . . or at least to one or two of them. So many of us live our lives with similar invisible burdens and hardships. Through Jesus we can learn from our past, live with purpose in the present, and anticipate the future. May the truths in this book be part of your process of becoming truly free and complete in Him as you contemplate the joy of becoming a spiritual mentor or being spiritually mentored.

Another traveler on the journey,
Ele Parrott

1

Jesus in every bite

I recently met Sandra for dinner and a talk at a local restaurant. We had never met before, but we had a mutual friend whom I have the joy of meeting with on a regular basis. Sandra had experienced a terrible weekend. She had just broken up . . . again . . . with her long-term boyfriend of six years. She had known for a long time that he wasn't "the one" for her, but he was better than no one, or so she had thought . . . until this weekend. Evidently, one thing had led to another and Sandra had finally had it with him. She had told him to "drop dead" and to never call her again, and she was dealing with the fallout of that decision.

Our mutual friend, Kristie, had called me on Sunday to fill me in on the situation. I was sitting in a church service when my phone rang. Yes, I know we're supposed to turn off our cell phones or put them on vibrate when we're in a service. But I've never figured out how to put my phone on vibrate, and I frankly had just forgotten to turn the thing off. So the phone rang, and I cut the call off immediately, telling myself that the disturbance was minimal and only a few people around me had heard the short musical calypso. But seconds later, it started beeping! Ah, the caller had left a message. Quickly digging the phone out of the too-small compartment on the side of my purse, I looked at the "missed call" list and saw Kristie's name. Uh-oh. I knew that if Kristie was calling me during a church service, it had to be important.

Whispering to my husband, Don, that I needed to take the phone call, I got up and awkwardly clambered over the others in our row to get to the aisle. Finally making my way out the door, I headed to the ladies' room to listen to the message. It was about Sandra. "Would you be able to meet with her soon?" Kristie requested urgently. "She's in a terrible state. She just broke up with her guy of six years." So there I was, two days later, at a Texas Roadhouse, munching on bits of an onion flower appetizer while listening to Sandra's story.

Sandra is a successful businesswoman. She has her own business and employs twelve people. She is the boss; she knows what to do and when to do it. She is known for being efficient and effective. She is successful . . . in that part of her life. However, in her personal life Sandra is sad, confused, angry, frustrated, disillusioned, and worst of all, alone. She allowed a guy to walk all over her, take advantage of her, live off of her, and repeatedly cheat on her. That's why she was sitting across from me sharing salted peanuts and an onion flower—Sandra was asking for help.

Because of the type of mentoring that I believe in, I didn't give her a list of things to do, which I could have done. I didn't recommend a book for her to read, though there are plenty. And I didn't tell her about my experiences of feeling lonely, confused, and devalued. Instead, I listened with intent interest, letting Sandra share whatever she wanted to share, in whatever way she wanted to share. I asked no questions; I simply listened without interrupting her flow of emotional thought.

Sandra spoke nonstop for nearly twenty minutes, sharing bits from the weekend's conversations with her now ex-boyfriend, some snippets from her childhood, memories of other breakups with this boyfriend, and a few stories about the resentment she felt growing up in Christian schools, before focusing back on what had transpired over the weekend. The entire time she talked I prayed for enlightenment, for understanding, and for direction from the Holy Spirit. "Jesus, who are You being in her life right now? How may I best partner with who You are in Sandra?"

When Sandra was exhausted from sharing, I thanked her for en-trusting me with her pain. Then I asked her a question. "Sandra, do you want a quick fix, or do you desire to be transformed by Jesus?"

For the first time in the conversation, I saw tears quickly well up in her eyes. She said, "Ele, I know a lot about the Bible. I have several Bibles at home all marked up with red, blue, yellow, and green colored pen-cils. I know the stories of the Bible. I can draw you a timeline of prophecy. But I don't know how to live life. I have no idea how to apply what the Bible says to my everyday life. How do I be a Christ-follower Monday through Saturday? Part of me wants the quick fix, but I know I need the other."

My response to her was, "Sandra, congratulations! You have made a wise choice. As much as you are hurting now, there is so much more of you that Jesus desires to embrace. Together we will begin this journey of knowing Jesus, for, you see, it's not *what* you know, it's *who* you know. What truly helps and fixes us is not the knowledge that goes in. It's about who lives life out through you—empowering you, cleansing you, and strengthening you. Jesus desires to be relevant in your life Monday through Saturday as well as Sunday. As you begin to discover who Jesus really is, this area of your life—as well as all areas of your life—will be transformed."

Sandra was voicing what many followers of Jesus sense, if not say. I hear it often. Let me try to put it into words: It's like people live their lives in separate sections or pieces, as if life were a bowl of fruit. There's a family piece, an employment piece, a friendship piece, a Jesus piece, and pieces for each other area of your life. Each of these pieces of life stay separate from one another, just as pieces of fruit in a bowl stay separate from one another. What goes on in the family piece has little or noth-ing to do with the employment piece, what goes on in the friendship piece is separated from the other pieces, and so on.

So when it comes to matters of faith, people who live their lives in pieces find it easy to keep their faith solely in their Jesus piece. One piece of life has very little to do with the other pieces of life. For example, if something comes up in the boyfriend piece, that piece of life is neatly removed, put on a plate, and fixed. Then that fixed piece is neatly put back in the bowl among the other pieces of life, with careful attention given to not disturbing any of the other pieces.

However, Jesus doesn't fit in a fruit bowl life very easily. While He lived here on earth, Jesus was the one who helped celebrate weddings, had midnight meetings with those seeking the truth, hung out at the local watering holes to rub shoulders with whoever was there, conversed with "religious" people, and played with kids. He literally permeated every part of a person's being when He was with them. Well, He's the same today. He's more like a cake than a bowl of fruit, so to speak. Let's think about that for a minute.

A cake is made up of flour, sugar, eggs, water, vanilla, baking powder, and various other ingredients. However, in order for the cake to be enjoyed as intended, it needs to be mixed—it requires blending. All the ingredients are still there, but each ingredient is enjoyed and experienced in *every* bite of the cake.

So it is with Jesus. When we spiritually mentor, we enter into a partnership with the Holy Spirit who has the potential to transform all aspects of a person's life. That doesn't mean that we try to fix certain quirks or focus on particular weaknesses or pains. As we partner with the Holy Spirit, we look for opportunities to infuse truth into reality in all dimensions of someone's life.

Using Sandra as an example, her reality is that the long-term relationship with her boyfriend is over. As a result, she is in pain. But that's only part of her reality. She is also a brilliant businesswoman, a loving daughter, a fun sister, a good friend, and a woman with desires, dreams, and ambitions. *All* of Sandra—every part of her—needs to be permeated by the Holy Spirit. Sandra is a woman who desperately needs Jesus in every area of her life. So to focus on just one area would deny the Spirit the opportunity to challenge and transform Sandra into the woman He desires her to be in every area of her life.

Let's get back to the question posed to Sandra. "Do you want a quick fix, or do you want to be transformed by Jesus?" Another way to put it is, "Do you want to be a bowl of fruit or do you want to be cake? Do you just want one piece of your life that includes Jesus, or do you want Him to invade and pervade all of your life?" One option is neat and tidy—no muss, no fuss. The other is messy, and it requires measuring, sifting, pouring, stirring, and the seemingly unbearable heat of the oven. Sandra's answer revealed her desire: she wanted Jesus. She chose the untidy and, at times, chaotic and painful invasion of her life by Jesus, who is "the way and the truth and the life" (John 14:6).

Sandra represents the kind of woman who responds well to being the mentee of a spiritual mentor. This type of woman hopes that there's more to being a follower of Jesus than what she is currently experiencing. She desires to be challenged and to be asked penetrating, revealing questions. She hungers for wisdom and inner strength. She wants to "go there" with someone whom she trusts to take her to Jesus. She's not satisfied with a quick fix, and she's willing to mix things up as needed. She wants Jesus in every bite of her life.

2

How to Begin
Spiritual
Mentoring
Part 1

Just Jesus
and you

How does someone become a spiritual mentor? Do you just hang out a shingle one day that says "Open for Business: Spiritual Mentor"? In some aspects it would be great if it were that straightforward and easy. But in the real world one does not go about spiritual mentoring in that manner. So what is the manner or method of becoming another person's spiritual mentor? It begins through *relationship* —relationship with Jesus, with our family, and with others.

The core of any relationship is your relationship with Jesus. It begins with you, with me, and with who Jesus is in us. We just can't give out more than we have ourselves. Don't get me wrong. Many do just that, and seemingly quite successfully. I am constantly amazed and disheartened by how easy it is for us to become orators of the Word of God. But I really don't see where being a spiritual talker is something to which we should aspire. In Scripture we read that we're not supposed to just be hearers of God's Word but also doers of it (James 1:22). I read nothing of us being "sayers" of the Word of God. That's easy . . . and that's *not* the stuff that a spiritual mentor is made of.

It begins in the quiet place. It begins with reading the Word of God for yourself every morning. It begins with a hunger and thirst after right living. It begins with a deep desperation in your soul that says, "Give me Jesus or I die!" It begins with a relationship between the Lord and you.

I distinctly remember when the Lord challenged me to "go there" with Him. The crazy thing about it was that I thought I *was* there with Him! Look at the facts of the situation: I had been active in my local church on a leadership level for over twelve years, I was married to a pastor, and together we were headed for the mission field as missionaries with our four young children. That had to count for something!

Language school was tough for us. It wasn't just that Don was in his early forties and I was in my midthirties. It wasn't that we didn't know any Spanish beyond Taco Bell, *burrito*, and *"¿Dónde está el baño?"* before we arrived in Costa Rica. It was a combination of several things. Up to that point in our lives, I knew who I was. I was a believer in Jesus Christ. I was a pastor's wife. I was a mother of four children. I was a leader in our church. When we arrived in Costa Rica, most of those "I wases" had been left on the shores of the United States. No one in Costa Rica knew that Don was a pastor. No one there cared that I was a mother of four young children, that I had led an entire children's program at our church, or that I sang in the choir. The main identity that transferred from one country to the other was that I was a believer in Jesus Christ. And that wasn't enough. I missed me. I longed for me. I needed me.

We made it through language school and eventually found ourselves disembarking from a jet onto the tarmac in Buenos Aires, Argentina—our new home. "Perhaps I can reinvent myself here," I thought. "Yes, that's it! I'll get active in our local church here in Buenos Aires and start all over again. I can do that!" With renewed vigor and high expectations, I made a list of everything that I had done in my "previous life" and made an appointment with our Argentine pastor. After all, I wanted to begin correctly, under the approval of our local pastor, and I figured he would certainly be impressed with my list of accomplishments.

I was ushered into Alberto's office for my appointment, and after exchanging greetings, I explained why I was there. I wanted to share with him what I had done in other church settings, and I desired to find out where he felt I could be of greatest use under his direction in that church. He listened with mild interest as I shared, in my best *castellano* (the Argentine form of Spanish), what ministries I had previously been involved in. At the end of my short monologue, I posed the question that would determine my place in my new home: "Pastor, how do you see me serving in this congregation?"

I had assumed that his answer would be prefaced by a rather long "thank you for blessing us with your presence and your abilities" speech, similar to the one my husband had received when he had asked the same question to the same person a few weeks earlier. I would then feign embarrassment and offer a bit of shy humility, perhaps, before accepting whatever positions he would bestow upon me. However, instead of presenting me with a verbal bouquet, Alberto leaned back in his chair, looked at the ceiling with great interest, and then uprighted himself again. He cleared his throat, looked me right in the eye, and said the words I will never forget: *"Los baños de la iglesia están sucios."* What? Had I heard him correctly? "The church bathrooms are dirty"? What did the state of cleanliness of the church bathrooms have to do with ministry? I was there to determine my next phase of helping others and he was talking dirty bathrooms!

Then it happened. It slowly dawned on me what Alberto was asking. Yes, you guessed it—he wanted me to clean the bathrooms! That would be my great, effective ministry for God in my exciting life as a missionary. He wasn't asking if I would organize and lead a women's Bible study, which I could do. He wasn't requesting that I gather the children together and start a kids' choir, which I would have loved. He wasn't even looking for input from me. He was stating a fact: the church bathrooms were dirty. What was I going to do about it?

I looked everywhere in the room except at Alberto. I had to think. I had to respond. I couldn't just continue to sit there with my mouth hanging open. So I did what any missionary worth her salt would do. I cheerfully said, "Hey, I have a super idea. Why don't I just take care of that little detail for you? It will be my joy to attend to those filthy bathrooms." Well, perhaps that's what I should have said, but in reality I looked him in the eye and said, "The bathrooms will be cleaned." In my heart I added, "I can't believe you are relegating me to that, especially when I'm qualified to do so much more. I'll show you! You'll have the cleanest, most hygienic bathrooms in all of Buenos Aires, in all of Argentina . . . and perhaps even in the whole of Latin America!"

Meanwhile, Don was having a great time in Argentina. He was invited to be part of the inner circle of men who ran the church. He was asked to preach on a regular basis. He was slated to lead worship, to direct the choir, and to do any number of other things to support the ministry there. His missionary experience and my missionary experience were very different, indeed.

Then something occurred that I never thought would happen to us. I became jealous of Don. I was green with envy. I could barely speak to him about his day without being sarcastic or rude. I hated myself, I wasn't thrilled with Don, and I was very, very angry with God. You see, I felt that God had tricked me. It seemed as if God had promised me one thing and delivered another. I felt bypassed, devalued, unnecessary, and lonely. And I didn't know what to do about it.

I was a follower of Christ. I was sold out to Jesus. I had given away nearly all of my earthly possessions. I had altered all my dreams for my marriage, my family, and me. I had gone through the embarrassment, the drudgery, and the pain of learning a new language at an older age. I had already paid my dues (hadn't I?), but I was being required to pay more. Why? Didn't those people realize how much I had adjusted my life to be there with them? And what would the folks back home think of this particular "ministry opportunity"? What a great prayer letter this would make: "Your missionary dollars at work: scrubbing toilets for Jesus!" It was all too much. My humiliation was nearly complete.

While God was humbling me, He was also systematically removing any and all support systems that I had in my life. The well-being of our children was in jeopardy. Our son was blackballed at his school for not knowing how to play *fútbol*, Latin America's word for soccer. Never mind that he was fun, witty, athletic, and willing to learn. He was rejected for not entering the system knowing all the ins and outs of the game. (By the way, he took it on as a challenge and eventually taught himself how to play.) Our youngest daughter began to systematically pluck out her hair, a sign of severe stress. Eventually she had pulled out all the hair on one side of her head. Such inner stress is something that a seven-year-old should never have to experience. I found another of our children in the fetal position one morning. "Mommy!" she screamed. "Turn the lights out; they hurt my eyes!" And that began months and months of her not eating, of extreme pain, and of going from one doctor to another specialist, only to have them say, "There's nothing physically wrong with her. It's all in her head." She slowly began to shrink away from all of us, withdrawing into a deep cocoon where she somehow felt safe. Another daughter had left behind friends, social position, and the promise of a very full and delightful childhood in the United States. In Argentina, she was wandering through a maze, trying to fit in and struggling to survive in this new world. I was losing my family, I had already lost much of my relationship with my husband, and I didn't trust God anymore.

God also quite purposefully removed any financial security we may have had. I remember that day as if it were yesterday. Two of the kids were enjoying the "fresh air" out on the minuscule balcony of our high-rise apartment in downtown Buenos Aires while the others were spending time inside with their visiting grandparents. When the phone rang, I answered it with my best *castellano* greeting. The voice on the other end of the line said—in English—"Hello? Hello? Are Don or Ele Parrott there?"

It was a long distance call from the States. Usually missionaries are glad to get such calls because it means that someone remembers them. But at that time we had come to dread those international calls. Time and again the callers were bearers of bad news. This time was no exception. The caller identified himself and in as few words as possible said something like this: "Sorry to have to tell you this, but at last night's World Impact meeting, we realized that we needed to cut back somewhere and . . ." In a nutshell, one of our supporting churches felt the need to cut back on the amount of money they were sending us. That was never good news, but at that particular time in Argentine history the cut was felt even more deeply because inflation was sweeping the nation in staggering percentages. So we were caught in the downdraft of other people's priorities and decisions and we had to live with it. No car for us; public transportation it was. No American schooling for our kids; the international school option was out the window. Our four kids would be taking the 82, a local public bus, to another section of the city where they would attend a local Argentine neighborhood school. We abruptly entered the world of uniforms, pledging allegiance to the Argentine flag, and studying English as a foreign language!

During that same time I was coping with my own lack of self-esteem, my anger with God, and my jealousy of my husband for his successful entry into the culture. I would frantically thumb through my Bible looking for help, for strength, for anything to help me stay afloat. I would pull out Bible study notebooks and begin to fill in the blanks, only to toss the book across the room, screaming, "What in the world does answering *that* have to do with what we're going through? Nothing!" I would pray and ask God to help me, to give me friends, to open up conversations, to do something . . . *anything*.

And then it happened. Instead of responding to me, God did the opposite. He became very silent. He stopped talking to me. And that scared me. God had always spoken to me through His Word. There was always a verse that would make it better. Except this time, there was silence and it was ironically deafening. I didn't know what to do. I would try to read and . . . nothing. I would try to pray and . . . nothing. I would try to journal and . . . nothing. I would take showers and cry my heart out to God, hoping that my family would think my puffy red face was due to the encounter with hot water. Fat chance. They knew. But they didn't know what to do; no one did. I was alone and I was petrified.

That's when Jesus stepped in, softly but deliberately. It was as if He was saying, "Ele, are you done now? Are you done trying to keep yourself sane? Are you done looking to others for help, for value, for purpose? Are you ready to begin with Me?" The crazy thing was that I thought I *had* "begun with Him." After all, what about all the years in ministry, the hours invested in women's Bible studies, the time spent with the kids' choir, the comings, the goings, the attendings . . . didn't they count for something?

Jesus quietly led me to the Word. He had me begin in the Psalms, and the washing of my mind with truth, the salve of His grace applied liberally on my emotions, and the unfolding of His glory and majesty began to transform me: my body, my soul, and my spirit. I became more and more hungry for His grace and truth in my life. He took me to the gospel of John, which began with "In the beginning . . ." What a great place to begin! I felt shy to be with Jesus. I had previously assumed that I had known Him, only to discover that I was perhaps meeting Him for the first time. I was drawn to Him like the women of old. I wanted to be with Him, to see Him, to hear His words, and to have Him touch me and change me. And He did. In the quiet of my innermost being, the Holy Spirit touched me through His living Holy Word and began to transform me from the inside out.

You see, Jesus' standard is for us to have a foundational, bedrock "I will die if I don't know You" type of relationship with Him. It's not about attending the latest workshop or Bible study. It's about Him and you—no one else.

Spiritual mentor, I don't know how He will take you to that point in your life, but He will. He will orchestrate circumstances, situations, personalities, and life issues; each time inviting you to allow Him to make you more like Himself. When He does that, grab on! Grab on and don't let go. Your hands will become bloody by holding on so tightly, but don't let go. You will cry with unbelievable pain of heart, but don't let go of Him. Persevere until His voice is heard. Hang on until His voice is recognizable. Don't stop until His voice is the one you desire above all other voices. Then and only then do you have a breath of a chance to have an authentic relationship with God. And no one else can do it for you; it has to be just Jesus and you. Period.

3

How to Begin
Spiritual
Mentoring
Part 2

Be Authentic
at home

*I*n the last chapter you were introduced to the idea of being spiritually authentic with Jesus. "Just Jesus and you" is the theme of that foundational thought. "Jesus and you" is core; it's foundational. There's no substitute.

The second nonnegotiable relationship in the life of a spiritual mentor is a healthy relationship with your own family. Let's take a look at what that relationship doesn't look like as well as what it does look like.

One of the first things that comes to mind for one who desires to be a spiritual mentor may be that having a healthy relationship with your own family members means you have to be perfect. That is simply not true. You need to let go of the idea that you can be perfect or that any of your family members can be perfect. You're human, your spouse is human, the kids are definitely human, and that's okay.

Interactions within your family will also never be ideal. You will not always communicate well. There will always be some misunderstandings among the kids. Your sex life might not always meet your expectations. Each member of your family most likely won't have their own devotional time every day or pray before eating. As you can see, "ideal" is closely related to "perfect." Neither of these models are what we need to have in mind in order to become qualified to be a spiritual mentor.

What we *do* need is authentic relationships with our families. Let me illustrate this by returning to the bathroom. Yes, I'm talking about the one in the church in Buenos Aires. If you recall, I was feeling quite devalued by our Latin pastor, who had asked me to clean the church bathrooms as my "ministry." With a very heavy heart and an "I don't want to do this" attitude, I went to the church building for my first cleaning session. As most women would agree, the preferred instrument with which to really clean very dirty bathrooms is an old toothbrush. So, there I was, in none of my glory, on my knees in the bathroom, scrubbing away with a toothbrush and trying not to cry.

"I hate this!" I told myself over and over. "God, how is *this* honoring to You?" My thoughts and prayers mingled as I was on my knees. Then, as can be expected when you're cleaning a semipublic restroom, women began to enter. "Oh, Doña Ele, why are you here cleaning?" they would ask. "This is my ministry," was my pat reply. At the time it seemed a little odd to me that the women accepted my answer. There was no, "But *you* shouldn't be doing that!" Neither did I hear, "Oh, let me do that for you!" It was quickly accepted as a fact that Doña Ele's ministry was to clean the bathrooms.

Girls would come in as I cleaned too. They would gather around, giggle, and then make small talk with me. None of it had to do with cleaning; all of it had to do with life, school, what happened on the bus ride to church, their friends, their fights, and so on. Among those girls were my own three daughters. They entered with their friends, chatting away, seemingly not bothered by the sight of their mom on her hands and knees, using one of their old toothbrushes to clean the toilets that they were about to use. Amazing. God was building relationships *and I almost missed it*—and three of those relationships were with my own daughters.

Before moving to Buenos Aires, I thought I had a good relationship with each of my four children. I would make sure that they were well fed, clean, clothed, and all the other things that moms take care of. I took them to T-ball, soccer, gymnastics, dance . . . all those "necessities" of life in our Western culture. They were also part of AWANA, the kids' choirs, drama, and anything else the local church had to offer. They got their schoolwork done on time and watched a minimal amount of television. Don and I had also purposed to make sure that each child had chores to do at home. So we were doing okay as a family.

The point I want to drive home about what makes vital and growing relationships with our family members is that we "are" with one another as opposed to "do" with one another. "Being" as a family is much different than "doing" as a family. Being means that there is communication among the family members that goes beyond "Mom, where are my clean clothes?" Being means that quantity as well as quality time is invested in those we love the most.

Being as a family also means that we act the same way with our families as we do in public. It's about authenticity. What's it like at your home? Do your kids see and hear one person at home and a very different one at church? What is your tone with them? How do you make decisions with and for them? What are you like when you're tired and just need time alone? Our kids see and hear us *always*. Others don't. How easy it would be to be authentic without a family! There would be practically nothing to it. But with our own flesh and blood . . . 24-7?

Ladies, if you don't have a handle on this part of your life, stop everything else you are doing. Resign from that committee, find someone else to play the piano, get a substitute to teach your class or Bible study, and then take care of business in your own home. The Enemy of our souls has a hold on a lot of us when it comes to this issue, doesn't he? Often it seems that we would rather give up our own family than let go of the limelight that teaching, singing, playing, and attending every meeting gives us. If that describes you, stop right now, get on your knees, and ask God to forgive you. Then get up off your knees, go to your kids, and ask them to forgive you as well.

We simply need to get things right at home before we should attempt to do anything outside of it. Do you realize that there is an increasing percentage of our children—the Generation Xers and the Millennials—growing up outside of the organized church . . . and many of them are believers? Why is this happening? They are sick to death of the hypocrisy they lived with and observed in the church as kids. Yes, they truly love Jesus, but they don't love His family as they have experienced it. If we desire to be effective as spiritual mentors, we *have* to be authentic with our own families—not perfect, not ideal, but authentic.

4

How to Begin
Spiritual
Mentoring
Part 3

Include others

After we have the core relationship established with Jesus and an authentic relationship flowing within our own family, we then need to include others in our lives on a spiritually significant level.

Let's return to the bathroom story one more time. There I was, on my knees, with women and girls entering the bathroom. Through that experience, God gave me the opportunity to be truly authentic with my daughters. But what about the others with whom I interacted?

What I hadn't realized up to that point was that it was going to be very hard to fit into that culture because there were several factors working against me—I was North American, I was white, and I had blonde hair and blue eyes. I had gone there to minister, and I wanted to fit in and be one of them, but I couldn't. They didn't want me, nor did they especially want what I had to offer . . . until they saw me on my hands and knees, cleaning their toilets with my old toothbrush. That one simple act put us on level ground. Because of the service I rendered them, they saw me as being approachable. I was one of them. I had been accepted, and God could begin to build on that.

The Holy Spirit took me to Philippians 2:3–8 one day. I had read that passage many times before, but that particular time I could hardly choke the words out because of the tears constricting my throat:

> Do nothing out of selfish ambition or vain conceit, but in humility consider others better than yourselves. Each of you should look not only to your own interests, but also to the interests of others. Your attitude should be the same as that of Christ Jesus: Who, being in very nature God, did not consider equality with God something to be grasped, but made himself nothing, taking the very nature of a servant, being made in human likeness. And being found in appearance as a man, he humbled himself and became obedient to death—even death on a cross!

I think I could feel myself grow a bit inside as I got it. God was gifting me with the privilege of being His servant to these dear people. He was using that silly old toothbrush in my hand to become a bridge by which I could enter the lives of the very people I desired to minister to.

Out of my personal tutorial under the Holy Spirit in God's Word, other women began inviting me to join them on their journeys. It wasn't long before some of the women from the church began dropping by our home for *merienda*, the early evening teatime. We would sit and chat as our children played together. The women would invite me to visit them in their homes as well, and soon we began sharing life with one another as women around the world tend to do. And when we were together, it just seemed natural to open the Word of God to get guidance on how to handle the various situations that popped up in our lives. We would pray and ask the Holy Spirit to teach us and to reveal truth to us.

Around that same time, our four children, who attended a local Argentine school, began bringing their friends home with them. I would be in the kitchen baking, so naturally the group of kids would gather in the kitchen. As they stuffed warm cookies in their mouths, there would be animated reenactments of school fights over which national soccer team was the best. Another day there would be a blow-by-blow account of how several kids in the class had been cheating on a test and how the teacher knew but didn't care. There would be talks about who liked whom, about homework, and about the injustice of everything. There would also be discussions about friendships, about parents, about siblings, about where we go when we die, and about God. During all those moments, I had the privilege of standing in the midst of those kids, serving them snacks, listening to them, and interacting with them. How thankful I was for those times with my children and their friends.

I was beginning to see how God was about *His* business, in *His* manner, for *His* glory. Women were growing in their faith. Kids were being exposed to truth as it related to the reality of their lives. And it all centered on God, not on someone's personality or gifting.

Eventually I was asked to write curriculum for families to use around the table as devotions, and I later wrote corresponding Sunday school lessons. Before long, the Lord allowed me to form a kids' choir, create a children's musical, and establish a puppet ministry. But all that came *after* those three core relational components—Jesus and me, authenticity at home, and including others in my life—were firmly in place, were being continually nourished, and were kept as a priority in my life.

You see, spiritual mentor, relationships are key. Relationships are vital. But they have to be the kind of relationships that are approachable, that are in "working clothes," that are honest, authentic, and growing. The core relationship with Christ has to be birthed in humility. This relationship has to be centered on Jesus, and Him only. Out of that core relationship comes an authentic relationship with our own family—those whom Jesus gifted to us so that we could first be spiritual mentors to them. And out of those two spheres of growing relationships, the Holy Spirit invites us to join Him in continuing relationships—coming alongside others in their journey.

I'm not advocating that everyone has to duplicate my experience. God is much too creative for that. If you are serious about having spiritual significance in the lives of others, God will find a way to make you hungry for Him, authentic at home, and approachable to others.

I recently received an email from a dear friend, Hope. Hope has a passion for Jesus. She wants her life to count for eternity, and she desires to have significant input into others' lives. Hope is also dying. I want to share her email with you to illustrate how God has put a toothbrush in her hands.

Dear friend,

Sad news today. I was just diagnosed for a second time with ovarian cancer. I don't know much at this point. We will be doing scans this week and an MRI to see how far it has spread.

Life is hitting pretty hard right now. But it doesn't sneak by our Father who knows and allows and loves and is with us through times like these. I was a bit weepy last night, but generally, I'm okay. The questions haven't changed from the first time, and neither have the answers. God is still God and works all things for the good of those who love Him. I love Him. But that doesn't mean I want to do this, though.

Pray for me, that I will "be Jesus" to the doctors, to other patients . . . to my own family. Pray for our kids, who watched a neighbor die of ovarian cancer last summer—a little too close for comfort. Our twenty-five-year old son in particular is at a very vulnerable place. He is still trying to make his faith his own, and at the moment, he seems to be listening to all the wrong voices. He's not sure that God is a God who interacts with us or is personal in any way. My prayer for him is embodied in the song "Draw Me Close to You." Pray also for my mom, who is about to lose her mom (my grandma) and who also is fighting to keep my dad on his feet. My dad has pancreatic cancer and emphysema. I'm probably my mom's best friend . . . you see the problem.

Holding on tightly to Jesus,

Hope

Do you recognize it? Do you see the old toothbrush in her hand? Do you visualize the dirty bathrooms that she is being asked to clean?

And what about you? What is your situation? What dirty bathroom is there for you to clean? Are you ready? More importantly, are you willing? Are you willing to pick up that old toothbrush, get down on your knees, and begin scrubbing?

God is looking for women who desire Him, women who long to be authentic with Him so that He can entrust deep relationships to them—relationships that invade another person's reality with God's truth. Are you ready to go there with Him? It may exhaust you. It may scare you. It may be painful, and it will certainly be lonely at times. But my advice is to stay with Him. Allow God to be who He desires to be in you so that you, in turn, may be all that He has in mind for you. In growing into that kind of believer, that quality of a follower of Jesus, you begin to qualify to partner with Him as He invades the lives of others around you. You have entered into the holy calling of being there for another who is on her journey with Jesus. You are becoming a spiritual mentor.

5

Mentor like Jesus

*I*f you are going to be a spiritual mentor, it would be helpful for you to have a formal definition of the concept of spiritual mentoring. So here is my personal definition: *Spiritual mentoring is coming alongside of and partnering with who the Holy Spirit is being in the life of another person and infusing truth into that person's reality.*

Let's take some time to really wrestle with this definition. It's not just a pile of words that were sorted out to make a sentence. I have thought, rethought, prayed, scoured Scripture, and asked the Spirit to teach me about this concept. Each word has been chosen carefully and purposefully. The rest of this chapter will be dedicated to unpacking this definition so that you can understand the significance of each word and phrase.

"Spiritual mentoring is coming alongside of . . ."

We see this in Jesus' life. He came alongside of people all the time. It's an interesting posture. Think about it: Coming alongside of someone implies that you are both going in the same direction. It implies that there is movement and action. It is not static; it's dynamic. It's messy at times. It's meeting people *who* they are, not who we would like them to be. Please overlook the clumsy English in the previous sentence, but this particular wording serves to drive home a point that is very important and freeing. Jesus could not have cared less about another person's job, position, appearance, financial status, social status, or anything else that made up his or her personal packaging—the "what" that so cleverly (or cruelly) covered the "who" of the person. He zoomed in on the "who"—the thoughts and intents of the person and the direction in which he or she was walking. He "came alongside of" those who were seeking truth, and He walked with them.

". . . and partnering with who the Holy Spirit is being . . ."

Consider this basic but profound statement: The persons of the Godhead are always partnering with one another. There is never conflict, never division, never strife, and never differing opinions among the Godhead. The Godhead is in perfect harmony with itself. We see this stated all over the Gospels. Jesus spotlighted this point with His disciples right before He offered Himself for our sins. Jesus told them that the Spirit was coming. "And I will ask *the Father*, and he will give you another Counselor to be with you forever—the *Spirit of Truth*" (John 14:16, italics mine). What a great example of the Godhead in harmony: Jesus is asking the Father to give the Spirit of Truth.

How does this apply to us? As followers of Jesus we have the Spirit of Truth living in us. We are told in John 14:26 that "the Counselor, *the Holy Spirit*, whom *the Father* will send *in my name*, will teach you all things and will remind you of everything I have said to you" (italics added). Therefore, it is to our benefit that we partner with who the Holy Spirit is being, first of all in our own lives, and then in the lives of those we spiritually mentor. And who is this Holy Spirit? The Holy Spirit is our Counselor, is Truth, is our Teacher, and is the one who reminds us of the things Jesus has said. The implication is dramatic. The implication is that we, then, are not the Counselor, we are not the source of truth, we are not the Teacher, and we are not the one to remind others. We are travelers on the journey—nothing more, nothing less. What a relief that is! We, as spiritual mentors, are in *partnership* with the Holy

Spirit. We are His junior partners. That means that we are ~~women of prayer and that we are women of the Word of God~~. It means that we are growing in our faith walk with Jesus. It means that we hear and recognize the Spirit's voice and respond quickly and appropriately not only in our lives but also in the lives of others. It means that spiritual mentoring is ~~not about us but about Jesus.~~

". . . in the life of another person . . ."

Jesus had parameters in His focus on relationships. His *influence* went way beyond His focus, but He did have a definite focus when it came to pouring His life into others. The Gospels mention that it was a fairly small group who traveled with Jesus. In that small group there were twelve who spent time with Jesus on a discipling or mentoring level—just twelve. And the implication was that only three of those twelve were in the "inner circle" with Him. Those twelve were the ones who lived and conversed with Jesus, who observed and questioned Him, and who absorbed the essence of who He is. The crowds certainly didn't. They were driven by self-centered expectations. "Feed us!" "Entertain us!" "Make our lives easier!" were the cries of the crowds. Jesus came and went among the crowds, but He stayed, He lingered, and He interacted with the Twelve. His heart centered on them. He was their spiritual mentor, and their lives were never the same after that as a result of who He was in their lives . . . and neither are ours.

To mentor as Jesus did is to focus on the life of another. It is to come alongside of someone, helping that person on his or her journey. It is not done by attending meetings, exchanging possible answers to filled-in blanks, or watching a teaching video. It is done one-on-one, life-on-life in the quiet corners of our very busy world. It is listening to another's story; it is pausing and musing over comments or questions that the followers of old also mused and paused over. Spiritual mentoring is desiring to be in another's life, not to change or correct her, but in order to lavish grace and truth on another weary traveler. It is to "be Jesus" in another person's life and leaving the outcome of that "being" in His very capable hands.

It is helpful to also look at the opposite of this part of the definition, "in the life of another person," which is "in the lives of lots of people." Spiritual mentoring, by definition, is *not* a group affair. Spiritual mentoring simply can't be done in a group atmosphere. Please be very clear on this point: Spiritual mentoring is done one-on-one. And what are the results? Lives are changed. Unholy patterns are broken. Minds are healed. Hearts are freed. Core cleansing occurs . . . one-on-one.

". . . and infusing truth into that person's reality."

Let's look at the word *infuse*. To infuse means to permeate, to saturate, and to immerse truth into something—in this case, into the life of another person. Truth is desperately needed in our world, where each person tends to live in his or her own reality. Each person's life is unique, with a distinctive personality, set of life circumstances, and experiences. A spiritual mentor needs to know the truth and then to know how and when to infuse that truth into the reality of the mentee's life. This cannot be done wholesale. Infusing truth cannot be done by attending Bible studies and sitting in a circle with other women. Infusing truth cannot be done by telling our story or by comparing our experiences with something that another person is going through. Infusing truth cannot be done by watching a DVD or by filling in blanks. Infusing truth into another person's reality can only be done by taking that person to Jesus. Infusing truth is done by partnering with who the Holy Spirit is desiring to be in the other person's life. It is done by active listening and by drawing on our own life experience with Jesus in order to form helpful and insightful questions for the mentee. Truth is infused by praying with and for the other person. Anything less is meddling, is assumption, is good intention. It is not mentoring.

You may have picked up that this definition of spiritual mentoring has no expectations attached to it. Our hope and prayer is that there will be change—that the mentee will desire to grow. But that is *not* a condition of spiritually mentoring someone. It is simply not our place to be the Holy Spirit in another person's life. Yes, we are to be concerned. Yes, we are to engage and think. Yes, we are to take her to Jesus . . . and then we are to *leave* her there with Him. I cannot stress this point enough. We are not our mentee's overseer or parent. We are simply another traveler on the journey of life who can help our mentee in her walk with Jesus.

As far as personal input is concerned, being a spiritual mentor is not about getting the chance to tell your story to someone else. It is not about imparting all your wisdom to a younger woman. It is not about finding significance by helping her or about identifying with how she feels or what she has done. Being a spiritual mentor is not about fulfilling your need to feel needed by someone or to be significant or popular with a group of women.

However, if the mentee asks for your personal input or opinion, then—and only then—should you give your input. You must keep in mind that you are partnering with the Holy Spirit in who He is being in the other person's life, and that you are striving to make her independently dependent on Jesus, not on you.

For some of us this is sad news. We want to be wanted. We need to be needed. It's a rush for us; it gives us recognition. We like being known as the wise one among the women because we're a spiritual mentor. When those thoughts enter our minds and begin to warm our spiritual bellies, we must counter them with truth. That's why it is paramount that we personally continue our daily journeys with Jesus. Otherwise we'll begin to believe the lie that we're important, that we're handling the reins in the other person's life, and that what *we* say is what matters. Scripture is abundantly clear on that subject. For instance, in John 3 we see John the Baptist's mentees getting upset because some of John's followers were falling away and beginning to follow this new mentor, Jesus.

An argument developed between some of John's disciples and a certain Jew over the matter of ceremonial washing. They came to John and said to him, "Rabbi, that man who was with you on the other side of the Jordan—the one you testified about—well, he is baptizing, and everyone is going to him!" To this John replied, "A man can receive *only what is given him from heaven.* You yourselves can testify that I said, 'I am not the Christ but am sent ahead of him.' The bride belongs to the bridegroom. The friend who attends the bridegroom waits and listens for him, and is full of joy when he hears the bridegroom's voice. That joy is mine, and it is now complete. *He must become greater; I must become less.*" (John 3:25–30, italics added)

We are "John" in the lives of the women who come to us to be mentored. They belong to Jesus, not to us. We "wait and listen for Him" and our joy is complete as our mentees step over the threshold in maturity and understanding, leaning heavily and deeply on Jesus . . . *not* on us. "He must become greater, [we] must become less."

The most effective tool to help someone else become independently dependent on Jesus is active listening, a tool that will be explained in detail in a later chapter. Jesus often used active listening in His interactions with others. For example, in John 1:38, we see Jesus turning around and asking His followers this question: "What do you want?" That is an incredibly great question. He didn't assume anything. He put no expectations on them. He simply asked an open-ended question, which is one of the hallmarks of active listening.

Take a look at the next part of this short conversation. "They said, 'Rabbi' (which means Teacher), 'where are you staying?' 'Come,' he replied, 'and you will see'" (John 1:38–39). What Jesus did here was incredibly wise. He offered an open-ended question, listened carefully to the answer, and then offered hope to His followers. To paraphrase what He said, "You *will* see . . . just come!" We can do the same with our mentees. As we turn around and see others behind us, we can offer them the same question, "What do you want?" Then after we carefully listen to the answer, we can offer them hope.

When we look at the following verses, we see the result of Jesus' invitation to "come."

So they went and saw where he was staying, and spent that day with him. It was about the tenth hour. Andrew, Simon Peter's brother, was one of the two who heard what John had said and who had followed

Jesus. The first thing Andrew did was to find his brother Simon and tell him, "We have found the Messiah" (that is, the Christ). And he brought him to Jesus. (John 1:39–42)

What an incredible outcome! As a result of spending time with Jesus, a man went and told his brother the good news.

Are you starting to realize the impact spiritual mentoring can have? Do you have an inkling how incredibly powerful spiritual mentoring can be? One of the first results of time spent with Jesus is that those in close proximity to Him want to share Him with those they love the most and then bring them to Christ or encourage them in their journey with Jesus.

Isn't that what we want as followers of Jesus? Shouldn't we desire to be with Him ourselves and then to appropriately share Him with others? I would propose that we have a viable, solid, God-given bridge with which to accomplish that purpose. It's not a program. It doesn't cost a penny to set up. No fancy building is required in which to meet. No extra materials are necessary. All that is necessary is Jesus, His Word, two fellow travelers, and time . . . nothing more. I invite you to start mentoring like Jesus. You'll never want anything else.

The Basic Difference
between Mentoring and Counseling

A question that arises quite often when I am speaking about spiritual mentoring is how it differs from counseling. To state the difference clearly and simply: Counseling is specific; spiritual mentoring is general. Counseling is focusing on a specific issue in a person's life and helping him or her work toward a resolution to that issue. Spiritual mentoring is walking alongside of another person in his or her spiritual journey with the focus on Jesus in their life in general. When something specific arises in the process of spiritually mentoring someone, if the issue can be dealt with in the light of the spiritual process, that's great. But if it requires more specific and professional attention, the person should be referred to a counselor.

So should spiritual mentors also counsel their mentees? If the spiritual mentor is also qualified to offer helpful counseling, then that skill and ability should definitely be available to the mentee. However, what we want to ensure is that the counseling doesn't override the spiritual mentoring. We must always keep in mind that the objective of any such relationship is to help the mentee become independently dependent on Jesus, *not* on us. We see this time and again in Scripture, where Jesus helps someone go from who they are to who they would like to be, but as a mentor, *not* a counselor. For example, when Jesus talked with the woman at the well, He sidestepped the many specific issues in her life in order to help her go from who she was to who she (and He) desired her to be.

Please understand that I have nothing against capable, qualified counselors. In fact, I am a Certified Biblical Counselor. I have also been told that I am gifted in sharing spiritual truths in a way that is helpful to the hearer. However, these tools *are not* necessary to be an effective spiritual mentor.

We will cover the three basic qualifiers of being a spiritual mentor in an upcoming chapter. Briefly, they are:

1. To be a woman of the Word of God
2. To be a woman of faith
3. To be a woman of prayer

These three qualifiers, combined with the skill of being an active listener and having life experience as a Christ-follower equip a woman of God to be a spiritual mentor. We see in Titus 2 that the invitation to be a mentor is offered in general to older women. In that context it was *assumed* that older women—the ones with Jesus-experience in their lives—would take on the mantle of mentorship, regardless of their spiritual gifting or other skills they may have acquired along life's path. Spiritual mentoring is an invitation for all believers, including those who are specially gifted or educated as a mentor or counselor. It is an invitation freely declared to all growing followers of Jesus as a fact, rather than an option. Spiritual mentoring helps us all transform together in Jesus!

6

Having the "right stuff"

Now that you know the definition of spiritual mentoring, let's look at what it takes to be a spiritual mentor. Not long ago, I had an email conversation with a woman about this topic. Perhaps reading our dialogue will give you insight about having the "right stuff" to be a spiritual mentor.

> Dear Ele,
>
> I've been considering how to be involved in ministry next year. While I wait patiently to see what God has in store for me when I finish my present responsibility, I'm exploring my options to maintain the greatest flexibility. At first I was excited about the idea of a new Bible study. I think I would love to participate in an evening group. I considered a couple of the various roles within the Bible study structure, but what has been laid on my heart is a role as a spiritual mentor. Do you think I have the right stuff to coach others in such a critical role? I would appreciate any honest suggestions you might have.
>
> Sincerely,
> Beth

Dear Beth,

It was with joy that I read your email. Your desire to be engaged in the lives of other women is commendable. You asked me if you have the "right stuff" to coach other women in such a critical role. That is a great question. The answer to your question actually has two parts. The first part of the answer pertains to the role of a spiritual mentor. The second part addresses whether or not you have the "right stuff."

First, let's look at the role of a spiritual mentor. We take our role from Titus 2:3–4, where we see "older women" teaching "younger women." This is a good example to follow, and it is seemingly simple at first glance. We see women who have experience in living life with Jesus interacting with women who are less experienced. However, it is necessary to pause and meditate on what teaching really means in this context. The most common approach to the concept of teaching in our modern Western culture is to talk—sharing facts and imparting knowledge from one person to another. We see this in education, in churches, and in business. It is a very common approach to the concept of teaching.

However, when we look to Scripture to see how Jesus taught, we see an entirely different model. We see a deep understanding of prayer, its purpose, and the power that lies within it as it is practiced. We observe time invested in the study and personal application of the Word of God. We notice Him spending hours with others in their comfort zones. We see time set aside with a select few for more private and intimate conversations. We witness Jesus, the master spiritual mentor, asking significant questions and then waiting for responses. We see life-on-life. We also see Jesus speaking to the multitudes from time to time. Yet the heart of His time on earth was invested in prayer, in "being," in interacting with people by asking key questions and waiting for their responses—responses that revealed their hearts and gave Jesus the opportunity to speak truth into their realities.

If I could summarize the word *teach* in the spiritual mentor context, it would be the following: *Earning the right to come alongside of another person in a spiritually significant manner and infusing truth into his or her reality.* Do spiritual mentors do this well all the time? Probably not, but it should be our objective. To be an effective spiritual mentor, one needs to be a woman of prayer, a woman of faith, a woman of the Word of God, a woman with good people skills, and a woman with time to earn the right to "be" in another's life on a significant level.

Now let's talk about whether you have the "right stuff" to be a spiritual mentor. A spiritual mentor (using the above standard) is in a season of life that requires less of her in her own sphere. Her children are grown or are old enough to allow her time to pray in depth, to be in the Word, and to give time to others outside of her immediate family. A spiritual mentor has a walk with the Lord that is growing, vital, and deepening. She has learned the arts of listening to the heart of the matter and of asking helpful questions that serve to clarify issues for the other person. She knows that sharing her own experience may, at times, be helpful, but more than that, she has developed the ability to present principles rather than examples.

I would encourage you to ask the Lord to place you with a godly older woman who would spiritually mentor you. Make sure that this woman is someone you respect spiritually and is also a woman with whom you easily interact. Learn from her. Observe her. Ask her to groom you in people skills such as the art of active listening. Invite her to help you feed yourself from the Word of God, and have her guide you in applying biblical principles in your life.

You have many skills, Beth. You are becoming who the Lord would have you to be; you are growing and maturing. I believe that the Lord may be grooming you in this area of spiritual mentoring. Give yourself the opportunity to be mentored first before you attempt to mentor others.

I would also encourage you to begin journaling or to continue doing it if you already do so. Write down what the Lord teaches you from His Word and lessons He has taught you in the past. Include struggles you have as a woman, a wife, and a mother. Record your inner thoughts, fears, and joys. Write down family situations, how they develop, and how they are eventually resolved (or not resolved). In doing this, you will be documenting Jesus in the daily process of raising a family and maturing as a woman of God in those surroundings.

Purpose to grow. Practice prayer. As you read Scripture jot down principles that jump out at you, and note where they are found in the Word. Be proactive in your own personal and family life in the application of those truths.

If I can be of help to you in any way, please let me know. You are an amazing woman. Keep on keeping on.

I hope these thoughts are helpful and encouraging to you as a woman, a mother, and a follower of Jesus Christ.

At your side,

Ele

THE CHARACTERISTICS OF A SPIRITUAL MENTOR

The recommendations I gave to Beth are only the tip of the iceberg when it comes to having the "right stuff" to be a spiritual mentor. There are several key components or characteristics that are necessary for effective spiritual mentoring. A spiritual mentor must be a woman of prayer, a woman of faith, and a woman of God's Word.

A *woman of prayer*

We all know that prayer is important, and this is perhaps best evidenced by the fact that Jesus often prayed. There are several things about prayer in Jesus' life that continually impress me.

I am impressed by the amount of time and priority that Jesus gave to prayer while He was here on earth. The priority that Jesus gave to prayer throughout His life is amazing. On many occasions, He would go off by Himself and pray. For example, "Very early in the morning, while it was still dark, Jesus got up, left the house and went off to a solitary place, where he prayed" (Mark 1:35). Jesus desired direct communication with the rest of the Godhead. He prioritized it over other relationships.

We also see that prayer for Jesus was a type of spiritual refueling. After the miracle of feeding five thousand men (plus women and children), we are told, "Immediately Jesus made the disciples get into the boat and go on ahead of him to the other side, while he dismissed the crowd. After he had dismissed them, *he went up on a mountainside by himself to pray*" (Matthew 14:22–23, italics added). What followed was another miracle of Jesus walking on the water and the subsequent miracle of Peter joining Him on the water, albeit for only a few moments. Tucked in between significant accounts of miracles, we see that Jesus purposed to get away by Himself to pray. Spiritual refueling was something that Jesus practiced.

Prayer was so important to Jesus that He took teaching time to instruct His followers on the importance of prayer. He told them how *not* to pray, and then He explained how to pray. We see this clearly in Matthew 6:5 when Jesus said, "And when you pray, do not be like the hypocrites." He described what a hypocritical prayer looks like and what the consequences of such a prayer would be. Then Jesus explained how we should pray. In my opinion, this sample prayer has been inaccurately called "The Lord's Prayer" when in actuality it would be better referred to as "the model prayer for Jesus' followers." That's not exactly a pithy title, but nonetheless, it seems to more accurately portray the intention of the prayer. Be that as it may, Jesus gave us this prayer so that our time invested in prayer will be effective and powerful. After all, James told us, "The prayer of a righteous man is powerful and effective" (James 5:16). I don't know about you, but I truly desire to be a woman whose prayers are powerful and effective. Otherwise, why pray?

Jesus also used prayer to bless others. Matthew 5:43–44 states that we are to pray for those who persecute us for His name's sake. There is much power released in this type of prayer. It grants the incredible release from hate for the person who is praying, and it allows God's perspective on the situation to be clearly seen. It literally infuses truth into reality in a tangible manner, freeing the one who prayed to be part of the solution rather than part of the problem. Also, in Matthew 19:13, we are given the account of Jesus blessing the little children by putting His hands on them and praying for them. What an incredible example that is for us not only as spiritual mentors but as mothers and grandmothers as well!

At times, prayer was a source of perspective and power for Jesus. Just before Jesus gave Himself up for us on the cross, what did He do? He prayed. In John 17, we have the transcript of some of what Jesus prayed in the garden of Gethsemane. (This, by the way, is the authentic Lord's Prayer.) We see Jesus praying for Himself, that He would be glorified so that He would glorify the Godhead. We see an amazing account of Jesus pouring truth into *His* own reality. That is a great example for us. How empowering that truth was to Jesus. It set Him free from the fear of what lay ahead for Him to the point that His prayer turned from a "help me" type of prayer to one that focused on protection for His disciples, *as well as* prayer focus on us—on "those who will believe in me through their message" (John 17:20).

We also know that Jesus utilized prayer as a weapon against the Enemy, Satan, and his demons. When the disciples were stumped by the fact that they alone couldn't drive out a demon, they asked Jesus, "'Why couldn't we drive it out?' He replied, 'This kind can come out only by prayer'" (Mark 9:28–29). Again, we see the importance of knowing how to pray effectively and powerfully.

This is not meant to be an exhaustive study on prayer. However, we can clearly see the importance and priority that prayer played in the life of Jesus, just from these few examples. What does that say to us about our own prayer lives?

Allow me to share with you an email conversation about prayer:

Dear Ele,

I have a question for you. This may sound weird, but is there any etiquette for praying? I guess I should ask if Scripture discusses this. I feel ridiculous about asking this, but thought I would.

With love,
Dana

Dear Dana,

I love your desire, your passion, your action, your thoughts, and your questions. God loves and delights in open hearts such as yours!

The question about "the etiquette of prayer" is an interesting one. We know that Scripture teaches that the prayers of *righteous* people are powerful and effective (James 5:16). Therefore, we want to entrust our requests to righteous people. So the question arises, "What is a righteous person?" A righteous person is one who knows who he or she is before God and lives according to that knowledge. In other words, a righteous person is a person of the Word of God, someone who lives the Word, one who lives her faith. A righteous person is one who is humble before God, dependent on God, and in tune with God. Examples from the Bible of righteous people are: Abraham (who lived by faith), Job (who suffered with understanding), Mary (who knew she was a servant of the Lord), and Lydia (who dedicated her business to God).

The most effective prayer is one that is aligned with the Father's will. His will is to make us more like Jesus. He accomplishes His will by introducing people, events, and situations into our lives, and by allowing us to choose Him over other options. For example, when someone contracts cancer, the first thing that comes to mind is to pray for healing. However, God's primary will is to use the cancer in that person's life to make him or her more like Jesus, and in the process, the lives of those observing how the person goes through the struggle are touched. John 9:1–3 illustrates this, "As he went along, he saw a man blind from birth. His disciples asked him, 'Rabbi, who sinned, this man or his parents, that he was born blind?' 'Neither this man nor his parents sinned,' said Jesus, *but this happened so that the work of God might be displayed in his life*" (italics added). Healing may or may not be part of the Father's will. So, an effective and powerful prayer would be something like, "Father, Jane has cancer. She's scared and she's wondering about a lot of stuff right now. We pray that the mind of Jesus will be in her and that Jane will walk through this life-threatening experience with dignity, focused on You and Your will for her. If healing is part of that, then we desire that. What we ask of You is strength for her day and for perspective and perseverance. We ask that You be glorified and that Jane be made more like Jesus, whatever *Your* will for her health may be."

Another way for us humans to communicate powerfully with our Father is to pray Scripture. Then we *know* we are partnering with what He would desire to see accomplished in someone's life. For example, "Lord, we know that Julie is holy and dearly loved by You. Clothe her with compassion, kindness, humility, gentleness, and patience. May she bear with her husband and forgive whatever grievances she may have against him. May she forgive as the Lord has forgiven her. May Julie put on love, which binds Bob and her together in perfect unity. And may the peace of Christ rule in her heart. May she be thankful, allowing the Word of Christ to richly dwell in her. May Julie be filled with wisdom. May she sing psalms, hymns, and spiritual songs with gratitude in her heart to You. May whatever Julie does or whatever she says be done in the name of the Lord Jesus. May she give thanks to God the Father" (adapted from Colossians 3:12–17). Now that's a powerful, effective prayer because it is the living Word of God being offered on behalf of the person being prayed for.

As you can see, praying is the most powerful tool we have as believers. We just don't get it, do we? It's like having an atomic bomb in our hands and playing with it as if it were a squirt gun. May you grow in your own understanding and usage of prayer, communicating with the Most High Supreme God, the Lord of all!

I'm very excited for you as you continue to grow in Jesus. May you be encouraged reading the Word and applying it by the power of the Holy Spirit as you become more like Jesus, day by day.

> Continuing to stand firm with you,
> Ele

A woman of faith

Another basic aspect of being an effective spiritual mentor is being a woman of faith. We read in Hebrews 11:6, "And without faith it is impossible to please God." That puts it plainly. Without faith it is *impossible* to please God. Perhaps it will help you, like it has me, to look at the opposite of that statement: *With* faith it *is* possible to please God. I like that!

The next step to figure out is how to be a woman of faith. What *is* faith? We see the answer in Hebrews 11:1, "Now faith is being sure of what we hope for and certain of what we do not see." In other words, we need to be women who step out boldly and confidently onto the *invisible*, not the *nonexistent*. To step out onto what is seen is a no-brainer. It requires no faith at all to just take the next step that you can see in front of you. And conversely, logic would say that to step out on that which is not there is foolish. However, to please God—to be women of faith—we must be so in tune with Jesus, so confident of who He is, so permeated by the Holy Spirit, that it is the *normal* option for us to daily take steps of faith.

How is this done? We find the guideline in the second half of Hebrews 11:6: "And without faith it is impossible to please God, *because anyone who comes to him must believe that he exists and that he rewards those who earnestly seek him*" (italics added). We live a life of faith when we believe that He exists and that He is exactly who He said He is, the Son of God, our Savior and our example. We live a life of faith when we earnestly seek Jesus by praying and by saturating our minds with the Word of God. We live a life of faith when we know that living for God is not a dead-end life.

God does not play games with us. There are rewards for earnestly seeking Him—seeking His perspective on life, seeking His strength to help us through our daily lives, and seeking His wisdom, just to name a few. If we desire to be spiritual mentors, we must be women who go to Jesus in prayer. We must be women who have a personal belief in Jesus. We must be women who know that He rewards those who earnestly seek Him. Jesus is not a manipulator. He greatly cares for us. He knows how difficult it is for a mere human to seek Him. That's why those who *earnestly* seek Him will be rewarded. He will reward *you* when you earnestly seek Him, and He will reward your mentees as you guide them to seek Him.

A woman of the Word of God

The third component of being a spiritual mentor is to be a woman of the Word of God. This may seem obvious, but the more that I interact with women who are followers of Jesus, the more I see that perhaps we're fooling ourselves a bit on this point. Let's look at this together. Scripture says, "Do your best to present yourself *to God* as one approved, a workman who does not need to be ashamed and who correctly handles the word of truth" (2 Timothy 2:15, italics added). The standard put forth for us is high: we are to present ourselves as one approved *to*

God. Again, what the text doesn't say is just as intriguing as what it does say. It *doesn't* say that we are to present ourselves for the approval of other believers. It doesn't say that we are to present ourselves for approval by attending the latest Bible studies, nor by filling out countless workbooks, going to numerous conferences, or watching Bible teachers on TV.

So what does it mean to be a woman of the Word of God? It means that we personally and individually open the Word of God and we ask the Holy Spirit to be our Teacher, which is exactly who He desires to be. We know this from Scripture. "And I [Jesus] will ask the Father, and he will give you another Counselor to be with you forever—the Spirit of truth . . . But the Counselor, the Holy Spirit, whom the Father will send in my name, *will teach you all things* and will remind you of everything I have said to you" (John 14:16–17, 26; italics added).

The pivotal question, then, is, "Who is my teacher?" In our Western culture in particular, we are inundated with options: what church to join, what Bible study book to use, what instructor to sit under, what conference to attend, what religious TV personality to send money to, and so on. However, none of those were even an option when Jesus was on earth. There were no churches, no study books, no biblical DVDs . . . nothing! Jesus could have presented any number of options to His followers about how to continue in the faith. He could have said, "Study with other believers in a church context." "Study under a famous Christian leader." "Study the latest Bible study workbook that comes out." Even though those things didn't exist yet, He still could have mentioned them, for after all, He is God! But with all the choices He knew we would one day have, *His choice was Himself.* John tells us, "As for you, the anointing you received from him remains in you, and you do not need anyone to teach you. But as his anointing teaches you about all things and as that anointing is real, not counterfeit—just as it has taught you, remain in him" (1 John 2:27). He wants to be your Teacher!

The Spirit desires to "teach you all things" (John 14:26). He's the One who will "guide you into all truth" (John 16:13). Why? *Because He wants the glory for Himself.* Jesus said, "[The Spirit] will bring glory to me by taking from what is mine and making it known to you. All that belongs to the Father is mine. That is why I said the Spirit will take from what is mine and make it known to you" (John 16:14–15). The Godhead wants to be glorified in everything we do. In 1 Corinthians 10:31, we are told that "whether you eat or drink or whatever you do, do it all for the glory of God." He wants earthen vessels, or "jars of clay" that will "show that this all-surpassing power is from God and not from us" (2 Corinthians 4:7). That's why it is so important that we are women of the Word of God ourselves, not merely products of another person's thinking and time with the Lord. The Godhead desires for us to be a class of one and for the Spirit to be our Teacher.

Was that hard for you to read? Do you feel like defending the Bible study class you're attending? Are you not wanting to throw away your tickets to the next Christian conference that is coming to town?

Here's my challenge. I place it at your feet simply for your consideration, if this part of this book is tough for you to read. My challenge is that you respectfully put aside all books about the Bible *except* your Bible for at least three months. Refrain from filling-in-the-blanks, from seminars and Bible studies, from TV teachers . . . as much as is possible for the next three months. During those three months, pick up your Bible, go to the book of John, and ask the Holy Spirit to teach you, to lead you into all truth, to help you rightly apply the Word of Truth. Then write down what is revealed to you in a journal. As you read, note the questions Jesus asked those around Him. Write down how He described Himself. Mark the reactions to Him, the comments made about Him, and whatever else the Holy Spirit impresses on you. Be strong in this. At first it may be tough to hear His voice; it may seem laborious or like nothing is coming through to you. Give yourself time. You may need to "detox" from hearing so many other voices. Gift yourself with those three months. Continue inviting the Holy Spirit to be your Teacher. You may be surprised at what happens. Chances are, you will never want to leave His classroom.

To whom do you want to present yourself for approval in your study of the Word of God? To God? To friends? To a certain woman teacher at your church, perhaps? Are you able to correctly handle the Word of Truth in your own life? Do you recognize the voice of the Holy Spirit as He attempts to teach you? The question isn't, "Do you have the right answers in the filled-out blank?" It's much more profound than that. If it were a matter of filling in the blanks, that would be a lot simpler than what the Godhead requires of us. But being a spiritual mentor —being a woman of God—is a high mark. It's not for the fainthearted. For He desires that we know truth, not facts. He invites us to study under the tutelage of the Holy Spirit, not under another human being. He yearns for us to become skilled in the application of truth in real life, on a gut level, not in a sugary-sweet superficial manner. God wants us to "shine like stars in the universe as [we] hold out the word of life" (Philippians 2:15–16) to those around us. With the Holy Spirit as our Teacher, we can truly "do [our] best to present [ourselves] to God as one approved, a workman who does not need to be ashamed and who correctly handles the word of truth" to our lives as well as to help others to become independently dependent on Him (2 Timothy 2:15). That is how we have the "right stuff" to become spiritual mentors.

7

Julie

She sat there across from me at Starbucks, holding her grande peppermint mocha. She had taken the lid off and she used a slim wooden stick to whip at the foam as she fought back tears. "He tricked me. While we were dating he said that he was a believer. We attended church together, sang the songs side by side, and took notes on what the pastor was saying. I bought it. I bought his act. Then something happened after we were married. Bob quickly grew uninterested in anything spiritual. He abruptly stopped reading the Bible, quit attending our Life Group, and started sleeping in every Sunday morning. When I question him about his faith, his standard reply is, 'Hey, stop pushing that on me. Back off!' Or what's even worse, he says nothing."

Julie is a slim, thirtysomething mother of three young girls. She has one sibling, a brother, who is serving time in a state prison. Julie's dad remarried when Julie was a young girl. She talks to her dad and his wife on holidays, and there are infrequent phone calls with her brother. Julie's mom stays in touch, but she's afraid of growing older, wanting to look and act more like a sister than a mom to Julie.

Julie's own life-mix is a jumble in and of itself. In her late teens and early twenties, Julie quickly became addicted to sex, any kind of sex, with anyone for any length of time. It wasn't unusual for her to have several relationships at the same time. Married, single, male, female . . . the whole gamut of sexual encounters was open to her. Along with the sex, Julie also became addicted to alcohol and she was a continual abuser of money, relying on others to bail her out.

Julie is a follower of Jesus. Her deepest desires are to be a woman of God, to be a strong godly wife, and to raise her three girls in a manner that is glorifying to God. Julie had little idea how to do any of that before I began meeting with her, but she started by attending Alcoholics Anonymous, which helped her tremendously. She has gone to "a higher power," whom she acknowledges as Jesus Christ. She has returned to others to make amends for the hurt, pain, and damage she caused in their lives. She attends AA meetings when necessary. But she still had little idea how to tap into all of who Jesus is and who He desires her to be.

Julie and I first met at a church gathering. When we spoke, she was articulate and to the point. "I want what you have with Jesus," she exclaimed at our first meeting. Evidently Julie had observed something in my life that was attractive to her. That "something," of course, is a growing relationship with Jesus.

Julie then inquired if I would be willing to mentor her. I told her, "Let's both take a week and pray about it. At the end of the week, call me and let me know what the Spirit has told you." She slightly tipped her head, looked at me with her green eyes, and agreed. We both went our separate ways, knowing that we would be in touch in seven days.

The follow-up phone call confirmed our prayers, so we met at Starbucks, where she confided in me about her marriage. I asked her, "Are you here to fix your marriage or to grow in Jesus?"

Julie stopped playing with the foam in her mocha and looked directly into my eyes. "I'm here to grow up in Jesus. My marriage is just one indicator that something is really off inside of me. I need Jesus to be real or I don't know what I'm going to do." Her desperation was tangible. She was serious. Jesus *had* to be all that He claims to be or she would be in real trouble . . . as well as her husband and those three girls. The same applies to her brother, her mom, her dad, his wife, her friends . . . for, you see, Julie's life is not just her own. Who she is affects others, and those others affect still others and so on. Jesus *had* to "come through" for her. And He has.

Since Julie had stated that she wanted to grow in Jesus, we pulled out our Bibles. We turned to John and I asked her to read John 1:1–18 aloud. She read, "In the beginning . . ." and then interrupted herself. "What a great place to begin to build a life—in the beginning!" The significance did not go unnoticed by Julie.

She restarted, "In the beginning was the Word, and the Word was with God, and the Word was God" (John 1:1). She went on to read, "In him was life, and that life was the light of men" (John 1:4). We talked about how Jesus is God. He is foundational in all—in creation, in relationships, in "all things" (John 1:3). Jesus contains life. He is more than life; Jesus is *beyond* life. "*In* him was life," the Scripture states (John 1:4, italics added). We talked about how Jesus is greater than life. Julie's perception of Jesus grew at that moment.

John continues, "In him was life, and that life was *the light of men*. The light shines in the darkness, but the darkness has not understood it" (John 1:4–5, italics added). Julie looked up from her reading. The words were not unfamiliar to her but the significance of the words was.

"Julie," I said, "let's talk about light in general. Light *is*. One does not have to conjure up light. It just *is*. Light, by just being, does one of two things: it reveals or it exposes. As you see who Jesus is in the gospel of John, He will begin to either reveal truth or expose areas of need in your life. That's who Jesus is: He's Light. What you choose to do with that Light is up to you. When something is revealed in you or about you, you have the choice to accept it and to agree with the Holy Spirit in what He is revealing to you. Conversely, when the Light exposes an area of need in your life, you will need to choose how you are going to respond to the area that's being exposed. Will you choose to go there with Jesus? Will you explore the exposure with the Holy Spirit as your Counselor and Guide? Or will you choose to brush Him off by ignoring or justifying the exposure? Remember, light *is*. What you do with the Light is your choice."

Julie paused to write something in her notebook about Jesus being Light. She then went back to John to discover how to have a personal relationship with the One who is beyond life. She read of Jesus, "Yet to all who received him, to those who believed in his name, he gave the right to become children of God" (John 1:12). She paused and I said, "Julie, tell me, according to this verse, how does one begin her life as a child of God?"

"Well," she began haltingly, "it says that you have to receive Him, and then believe in His name, and then He will give you the right to become children of God."

I confirmed her answer and continued, "I have a question for you to think about this week. Are you a child of God and, if so, how do you know?"

"Oh! I can answer that right now!" exclaimed Julie.

"I'm sure you can," I responded, "but I would like you to take time to think about your answer. Ask the Holy Spirit to reveal truth or expose a need in your reality about this. Then write down what He tells you."

"Okay, I can do that," was Julie's reply.

She began reading again, "The Word became flesh and made his dwelling among us. We have seen his glory, the glory of the One and Only, who came from the Father, full of grace and truth" (John 1:14).

"Let's pause there a minute, Julie," I said. "I have a question for you: What is Jesus full of?"

Julie laughed. "What? What a question!"

"Yes, it is," I agreed, smiling. "The verse says He is full of something. What is Jesus full of?"

After a brief pause Julie answered, "It says that He is full of grace and truth!"

"That's right," I affirmed. "Jesus is full of grace and truth. Let's talk about that for a minute. The Godhead could have chosen any number of words to describe Jesus, but the two words that were chosen were *grace* and *truth*."

"That's impressive to me ... grace and truth. So, what do those two descriptors mean?" Julie asked.

I answered, "The most down-to-earth explanation of grace that I know of is the following: Grace is giving what is not deserved. Can you relate to that? I certainly can. Jesus gives you and me what we do not deserve. Thank God for that! If we received what we *did* deserve, we'd *both* be in a world of hurt. The book of John will help to flesh out more about grace as we unfold who Jesus truly is.

"So what about truth? Basically, truth is the total absence of any shade of falsehood. It means no lying, no fudging, no covering up; truth means being totally genuine, absolutely accurate, and unswervingly exact, with perfect precision. Truth is God's reality. We see in John 14:6 that Jesus says *He* is the truth. He doesn't just contain truth, He is the very essence and the source of truth. Jesus is God's reality—truth—for us in our world.

"Another interesting point about these two descriptors is their order. You see, the text could have been written, 'full of *truth* and *grace.*' But we see in verse 14 and in verse 17, 'grace and truth came through Jesus Christ,' that *grace* leads *truth.* That's Jesus. Grace—giving what is not deserved—always leads truth—accuracy, exactness, and complete honesty. Grace is the gentle path on which truth enters our life. Jesus is just that: He is the way that fleshes out truth that leads to life, and not just any life but abundant life!"

Julie sat there soaking it in. That was a lot to receive. There was much to think about. And our first time together was just about over. "Julie," I said, "during the week I would encourage you to read and reread these first eighteen verses of John. Invite the Holy Spirit to continue teaching you. Allow His grace to prepare a path on which truth may enter your life. Also, I'd like you to jot down a few questions to think about and answer for our next time together." The questions are below:

- ❖ How does one become a child of God?
- ❖ Would you say that you are a child of God? On what do you base your answer?
- ❖ What are *you* "full of"? Ask your husband and a few of your closest friends and or relatives to give you two or three words that describe you. Write down their responses.

- ❖ What would you like to be full of? Ask the Holy Spirit to help you on this one. Write a few things down, leave it, and then come back to it, adding or subtracting ideas as necessary.
- ❖ Write down anything else you want to share or discuss from these verses.

I finished by giving Julie some words of encouragement and by asking the Holy Spirit to continue to be her Teacher. She smiled, put her Bible and notebook in her bag, and quickly finished her then cold peppermint mocha. Putting the slim wooden stick in the stiff paper cup, Julie tossed it away as if she were tossing away an invisible burden . . . for she was. Julie was on her way to "becoming more like Jesus" with Jesus Himself—the Light, the Grace-Giver, the Truth. And that gives her hope for her life.

8

Step by step by step . . .

As I travel around to conferences and retreats, I'm asked to share the steps a spiritual mentor would take in order to begin and continue a spiritual mentoring relationship. What I'm going to share with you in this chapter is one option for the process of spiritual mentoring, and it's one that I know to be very effective. Let me be clear that I realize there are a variety of ways in which spiritual mentoring can occur. There is no one right method; the Holy Spirit can work in a variety of ways. However, this approach has worked for me, and I believe it is both helpful to the mentee and honoring to the Holy Spirit. Join me as I go through the basic components involved in my time-tested process of spiritual mentoring.

Ask for Guidance

The first thing you need to do is to pray. Ask the Holy Spirit if you are ready to be a spiritual mentor. Not everyone is. You might still need to be mentored by someone else, depending on where you are in your relationship with Jesus. Along with prayer, you will need to continually feed yourself from the living Word of God. Nothing takes the place of having the Holy Spirit teach you, counsel you, and guide you.

RESPOND TO THE SPIRIT

After you have prayed and sought the Spirit's counsel, respond appropriately by accepting His guidance, whether He tells you to move ahead or to wait. Continue praying and growing yourself, not seeking the position of mentor, but being willing to wait as the Holy Spirit leads you.

PRAY FOR CONFIRMATION

When approached by someone who wants to be spiritually mentored by you, thank her for the honor, ask her to pray about it for a week, and tell her you will be praying as well. During that time, ask the Lord to confirm His will in both of your lives.

It may seem as if I missed a step—the one where you actually find someone to mentor. But I am a believer in having the potential mentee approach you instead of you approaching her. When someone approaches you, it is an obvious statement of trust in you; it conveys her desire to confide in you and to let you "invade" her life.

Even though you're not actively seeking out a specific person to mentor, you can make it known that you are open and available for such a growing, dynamic relationship. There are a variety of ways this can be shared. For example, if you have been involved in a parenting organization such as MOPS, you might let them know that you are willing to mentor a young mom. Just work through your circles of influence to let others know of your desire to be a spiritual mentor.

Sometimes mentors and mentees are paired up in a large group setting. I would counsel against this because this method runs the risk of placing people in an uncomfortable position. The mentee might end up not wanting to meet with the mentor (and vice versa), but just not know how to get out of the imposed arrangement. This is not the best way in which to begin a relationship. And that's what mentoring is—a relationship, not a project or a program.

Step by step by step . . .

MEET ONE-ON-ONE

When the Holy Spirit confirms to both you and your mentee that this is a relationship He desires for you, it's time to arrange your first one-on-one meeting. Your mentoring times should always be one-on-one. Why? When you mentor someone, you are establishing a spiritual relationship with another traveler, and spending time with only that person is necessary to allow the relationship to grow. Keep in mind, this is not a Bible study or a meeting where you are initially in a large group and then break off to talk in pairs.

Another reason why this time together needs to be one-on-one is that trust needs to be established and then maintained. Women gift one another with trust quite readily. It is the exception to the rule to have to earn someone's trust. However, almost just as easily, women tend to break each other's trust. This is painful, damaging, and, frankly, un-necessary. When you confine your meetings to just you and your mentee, trust has a chance to grow and develop in the fertile soil of a Christ-centered relationship.

INVEST SUFFICIENT TIME

Dedicate a lot of time to your mentee. When spiritual mentoring is based on a relationship, time is required to flesh it out. Don't base the amount of time you spend with someone on the length of typical meet-ing times, such as an hour each week. You will need to invest quite a bit of time in the women you mentor. People require time to share their stories. Women need time to "unload" so that they will then be ready and willing to receive what you have to give them. This time needs to be protected. By that I mean that this time needs to be taken somewhere away from her work environment, her home, and her husband. This is *her* time, dedicated to *her* growth as a follower of Jesus. However, at times I find that meeting with moms with young children requires more flexibility. They are so appreciative of a mentor who can be flexible with them. I do meet with some of these women in their homes. They put their children down for a nap or have them watch a video so that we will have time together to share, discuss, and grow!

Remember not to rush your mentee as she is sharing. (Please refer to the chapter on active listening for more details.) Also, avoid the temptation to talk about yourself. Most people—especially women—are desperate for someone to listen to them, to hear their heart, and to ask them clarifying questions. So take your mentee to Jesus and stay there with her.

Just as an example, I set aside two hours for each time I meet with each woman I mentor, and we never have trouble filling the time. You don't have to follow my lead on this; simply figure out what amount of time works best for you and your mentee.

BE PREPARED

Have your mentee bring her Bible, a notebook, a pen, and her calendar every time you meet together. You will also need a Bible, your notebook of what the Lord is teaching you, and your calendar. Having these items in front of you will help you focus on the task at hand instead of on idle chitchat.

The uses of all of these items may be obvious, but I'd like to go into a little bit more detail. As you can guess, the Bible is to be used for reading purposes. The notebook is useful for the mentee to take notes, to jot down questions, and to refer back to previous conversations and meetings. Having a pen guarantees that what needs to be documented will be documented. And the calendars will give the two of you the opportunity to plan your next time together. I find that few women have the luxury of meeting at a regularly scheduled time. Flexibility is important, and having your calendar with you ensures that you can find a time when both of you can meet. It might be helpful to try to work a month in advance. I try to meet with each mentee every ten to fourteen days. Meeting every week seems a bit much and any longer than two weeks between meetings seems too long. The goal is to be flexible.

CHOOSE WHAT YOU WILL STUDY

You will need to choose a book of the Bible—*not* a topic—to study. My suggestion is to begin studying "in the beginning" in the book of John, because Jesus is very approachable in that book. However, please don't limit yourself if the Spirit is leading you to another book in the Bible. My mentees and I have had great experiences with Nehemiah, Jonah, Proverbs, Galatians, Ephesians, and a number of other books. When you first start to meet with your mentee, it is best for *you* to choose which book to study. After that, you will probably want to make a joint decision with the person you are mentoring.

LET THE MENTEE SHARE

After settling into your meeting space, remind yourselves that the Holy Spirit is already with you and will be involved in the conversation. Thank Him for being a Teacher to both of you. Then ask your mentee, "What's going on in your life?" Trust me when I tell you that's all you will have to say for the next twenty minutes. Your mentee will be ready to share, especially if you have set the pattern of active listening with her. Engage in what she is saying, always looking for the Holy Spirit's handprints in her life. This will become the hallmark of your time together—helping her see the handprints of the Master all over her life. She will be eternally grateful to you for this.

STUDY GOD'S WORD

After your mentee has had a chance to share, she will be ready to receive wisdom and guidance from the Teacher—the Holy Spirit. You will know she is finished sharing when she begins to slow down, repeat herself, or actually stop. Always say, "Is there more you would like to share?" This gives your mentee the invitation to continue if there is something she would like to share but is hesitating to do so.

When your mentee is done sharing, invite her to read the portion of Scripture that you have chosen for her to study. (Note: Make these portions smaller, rather than bigger. In our Western culture we have mistakenly equated "big" with "better." That's not necessarily the case in our spiritual lives.) Scripture exhorts us to "meditate on [God's] precepts" (Psalm 119:15) and to "think about such things" (Philippians 4:8). This requires little bites . . . small portions. Start and end with the same account, the same thought. Don't attempt to combine Bible passages or concepts. You're not in a race; you're in the relationship for the long haul, just as Jesus is with us.

Let me walk you through my approach to studying Scripture in a mentoring relationship. First of all, think about the significance of Bible passages and stories. Out of all the people who have ever lived, walked, and breathed on this earth, God chose to document a few of their lives. Why did He do this? He wants us to learn something from each of those lives and situations. Our challenge is to discover the reason why God chose to document those particular people and moments in time.

With that understanding of Scripture as a backdrop, invite your mentee to read the portion of Scripture out loud. I find that there's something powerful about hearing the Word of God read aloud, and it's great to hear the Word of God proclaimed in a public place, if that's where you're meeting.

Let's use John 5:1–9 as our sample of a short Scripture passage to study. This is a familiar passage—the one that records Jesus having an encounter with a man who had been sick for thirty-eight years.

First, ask the mentee to read John 5:1–9 aloud. The first thing that jumps off of the page is the posture of the man. He is "lying there" (John 5:6). The second noteworthy detail is how long he had been lying there: thirty-eight years (John 5:5). The account goes on to say, "When Jesus saw him and knew he had been ill for a long time, he asked him, 'Would you like to get well?'" (John 5:6 NLT).

Jesus asked a question that would seem to have an obvious answer: "Would you like to get well?" But notice how the man responds. "'I can't, sir,' the sick man said, 'for I have no one to put me into the pool when the water bubbles up. Someone else always gets there ahead of me'" (John 5:7 NLT) Did you notice what he did? He gave an excuse . . . and then he blamed others. But that wasn't the end of the story. The account goes on to say, "Jesus told him, 'Stand up, pick up your mat, and walk!' Instantly, the man was healed!" (John 5:8–9 NLT).

What do you see in that passage that you or your mentee can relate to? What did you feel as you read it? Is there anything there that's applicable to your mentee?

GLEAN FROM THE TEXT

Note that while the John passage is a short one, there is much truth to be gleaned from those few verses. The idea is to start gleaning observations and questions *from* the text, not *about* the text. There is a huge difference. Your motivation is to absorb what is being said. You want to "crawl into" the text and see it from every experiential angle.

Still using John 5:1–9 as our example, what are some observations and questions you and your mentee can pull from this text? As previously noted, the first obvious observations are that the man was disabled and that he had been lying by the pool for thirty-eight years. What does this have to do with your mentee? She may not be physically disabled, but she may be spiritually, emotionally, or socially disabled. In what ways is she "blind, lame, or paralyzed" (John 5:4 NLT)? How long has she been "lying there," waiting for someone else to help her?

The next thing we observed is that Jesus entered the man's life and asked one question, "Would you like to get well?" (John 5:6 NLT). Jesus is asking your mentee the same question, "Would *you* like to get well?"

We notice that the man then did a very odd thing. Instead of giving a resounding, "Of course!" he said, "I can't" (John 5:7 NLT). Do you sense something similar in your mentee's life? Do you feel the doubt, see the fear, or notice the disbelief? If so, ask her! Ask your mentee the same question that Jesus asked and then wait for her answer.

The intent of spiritual mentoring is to flesh out the "how" of being a follower of Jesus. We usually understand without too much effort the "what" of being a Christ-follower. But the "how" is a different story.

Our objective as spiritual mentors is to help our mentees discover how to put Jesus in their everyday lives.

Digging into God's Word in this way takes us from a one-dimensional Bible study to a multidimensional, vibrant, daily discovery of the Living Word of God. So ladies, start digging! Pick up your spiritual shovel and start excavating the holy and precious Word of God. Throw a pick to your mentee and have her start mining as well. You are in a deep quarry and you will turn up all sorts of incredibly valuable finds placed there just for you from Jesus—the Creator of Life!

RECORD THOUGHTS AND QUESTIONS

As you study God's Word, have your mentee write down any questions, thoughts, or insights she has. Remind her that the Holy Spirit is her Teacher, not you. Encourage her to take time each day to talk to Jesus about why He chose to document the passage you read. Prompt her to invite the Holy Spirit to teach her what He wants her to learn from the passage and what can be applied from the passage to what is going on in her life. Then have her jot down what she senses the Holy Spirit is showing her. Encourage her to return to her answers throughout the week. Perhaps what the Spirit will show her on Monday will only be a prelude to the depth He will reveal on Thursday. Give her the freedom to adjust, add to, and edit the musings in her journal. Discussing what she writes down will make up part of the time you share with your mentee each time you meet.

End your time together by thanking the Spirit for His constant presence and His desire to continue to help both of you become more like Jesus. Then get your calendars out and mark down the next few times you will be meeting.

As you can see, the process of spiritual mentoring is fairly simple and straightforward. All of us can follow these helpful steps. And we can all dig into God's Word with the Holy Spirit's help. So dig in, spiritual mentor, and encourage your mentee to do the same. Will there be times when you feel like you're stuck? Yes, there will be. Will there be times when you don't get it? That is a guarantee. But will there also be times of deep spiritual insight? You can count on it!

May we choose to walk step by step by step with Jesus as we come alongside of others on their journey with Him.

9

Tara

Tara's short brown hair is cut in a sensible, no-nonsense style. She leans forward when she walks as if the incline of her posture will help to get her to her desired destination quicker. Her deep hazel eyes are penetrating, reflecting intelligence and a bit of skepticism. Tara is a recovering alcoholic, a definite workaholic, and a leader in whatever situation she finds herself . . . except one.

Tara is a follower of Jesus. She has been for years. Tara has taught other women using different Bible study books. She has frequented countless women's spiritual life conferences, gone to workshops on the Christian life, attended weekend spiritual retreats, and has listened to countless cassettes and CDs on "how-to" *everything*, and all according to the most current popular Christian "guru." Tara knows a lot about the ins and outs of the organized church. She has sat on almost every committee there is, and she currently chairs the outreach committee of her local church. Yes, she knows church; but she has little idea who Jesus is. That discrepancy really irritates her. It should. After all, having a working understanding of the organization of a local church and being in a vital relationship with Jesus are two very, very different things.

Until recently Tara was very satisfied with her life. It was all organized how she wanted it to be in a fruit bowl life. In the family piece of life, she and her husband of twenty-plus years are still in love with each other, and her three nearly grown children are all doing reasonably well. Her business piece of life has never been better. Tara began her own house-keeping business when her kids were small. Now she has crews working for her and she is the manager. Tara, with her to-the-point personality, manages well, and her business is thriving as a result.

The friend piece of life has always been "interesting" to Tara, to use her word. She chooses friends whom she can dominate, ones who need her. Her friendships are usually as deep as what a game of Bunko and taking in a movie will allow. She has lots of friends but few, if any, deep relationships. She rarely misses her Alcoholics Anonymous meetings. She mostly listens, but she shares occasionally when life gets a bit too heavy for her to bear. She knows the importance of keeping herself sober, and she relies on those AA meetings to defuse her as necessary.

Tara's church piece of life is full of attending many meetings, chairing various committees, and going to any event she can. This piece of her life had been satisfying to Tara, up until now. It is interesting to Tara that she would not use the word *fulfilling* to describe the church piece of life. Nothing really fulfills Tara. She's a realist and doesn't expect the "glass" of life ever to be full. To be half full is as good as it gets . . . and yet, there's something within Tara that wants more, that desires more, that anticipates more.

That "something" is what led Tara to call me. I was surprised to receive that phone call from Tara. I had seen her here and there at church, always surrounded by people, always involved, and busy rushing from one group of people to another. She would say something to the group and all of them would put their heads back in unison and laugh as if on cue. Tara knew how to work a crowd. People liked to be around her. She "raised the bar" wherever she went. Tara was in control and had it all together, whatever "it" is. So when Tara called and asked if I had time to get together with her, I was surprised. And I have to admit I was also somewhat intimidated. Why would a woman such as Tara be calling me? Did she want to recruit me for a committee she was chairing? Did my name come up in some conversation? Was I in trouble? My mind ran rampant with the possibilities. However, I agreed to meet with Tara, mostly out of church courtesy. I was not particularly looking forward to it.

We met where countless business or church encounters take place, at a Starbucks. I ordered my usual grande soy, no water, no foam chai. I was feeling quite righteous in my healthy choice of soy when Tara ordered a green tea. Green tea? She chose a drink with absolutely *no* calories that is actually good for you? At that point I really did feel intimidated . . . and I hoped my drink choice wasn't part of my interview for whatever committee she wanted me to join! But in spite of failing the "order test," I decided to do my best to enjoy getting to know her.

Since Tara had called the meeting, I waited for her to begin the conversation. What she said caught me off guard. "Ele, I know that you meet with Julie. We know each other from church and from our AA meetings. She told me that you're meeting with her and she called you her spiritual mentor. What in the world does that mean?"

Still not knowing exactly what she wanted from me, I gave Tara my quick textbook answer. "To me, being a spiritual mentor to someone means that I earn the right to have significant input in her life by partnering with the Holy Spirit in who He is being in her life. I come alongside of her, and, as we study the Word of God together, I help to infuse truth into her reality with the objective of her becoming more like Jesus." Then I steeled myself against whatever the fallout of that hurried explanation would be.

Tara's response surprised me. She leaned forward in her chair and declared, "Now that's the most interesting and cool thing I have heard of in a very long time! Where did you get such an idea as *that*?"

I explained to Tara that, after saturating my mind with the gospel of John for several years, that was the example that I saw in Jesus' life while He was here on earth. He never imposed. He was always compelling. He spent time with people, earning the right to have significant input into their lives. He definitely infused truth into the realities of *anyone* who invited Him to invade their lives: blue-collar workers, government workers, mothers, religious leaders, children, and business owners. Any and all were welcomed to "go on the journey" with Him. Few accepted, but the ones who did were the ones whose lives were never again the same. When Jesus truly entered a life, that life was transformed from the inside out—every aspect of it. I went on to share how that same invitation is still extended to all of us who follow Jesus now. He desires so much more for us than we can ever think, ask, or imagine!

I guess I was still waiting for Tara to nail me on something, but what happened next changed my perspective. Tears began streaming down her cheeks. She didn't try to hide them or wipe them away. She let them run down her cheeks and trickle down her neck. She was oblivious to them. "Why haven't I met *this* Jesus before? Where has He been? What have I been doing all these years? Are you sure this is true? I've attended church since my early college days; I've gone to seminars; I've attended conferences and workshops. I've even led the women's Bible study and was quite a popular teacher! I'm currently on a committee at church; in fact, I'm the chairperson for it. But what you've said in the last five minutes is rocking my world!" She paused, looked down, and then quickly looked up again with determination in her eyes. "If this is true . . . wait . . . if *half* of this is true, I want it! I want it all! I want it all, right now!" she exclaimed as she beamed at me.

Well, it is true. *All* of it is true, as Tara began to discover for herself. We went to John and started "in the beginning" (John 1:1). She loved everything about reading John (though she had read it many times before) and discovering the truth that is there. She delighted in reading about Jesus—that He is "full of grace and truth" (John 1:14). She nodded with understanding and appreciation when we discussed how grace goes before truth, and that grace is the gentle path on which truth enters our life. She wrote down ideas, marked verses in her Bible, and almost continually asked, "Why haven't I heard this before? I've even *taught* this before and didn't get it!"

What's intriguing about Tara's journey is that she quickly invited others to join her. Some of those "others" were her own kids. Being the practical, type-A person that she is, Tara made appointments with her three teenage kids. She sat them down, explained to them about what was going on in her own life, and then opened up her Bible to John and started "in the beginning" with them. When she told me what she was doing, she was animated. "Ele," she began, "you ought to have been there. It was a riot! When I asked my kids what they were full of, you know, after reading how Jesus is 'full of grace and truth,' they just howled! They really got a kick out of Jesus being 'full of' something. You know kids. Anyway, after the joking was over, that question got them thinking, 'What *am* I full of?' It turned into the best discussion our family has *ever* had! This is so cool! Why haven't I heard this before?"

Tara is also learning how to "be" Jesus for her growing children. She has shared with me about how she often tried to fix things for her kids; how she tried to relate to them and give them options to help them solve their problems. "How is that method working for you?" I inquired one day.

"If the truth be known, not so hot. They start rolling their eyes, looking like they're about to throw up. All I want to do is to help them, to relate to them. They just don't understand," she explained.

"You're probably right," I replied. "They don't understand yet about how much you really do love them." I paused. "Perhaps there are other ways you can help them."

"Like what?" Tara wanted to know.

"Well," I began, "it's interesting to note how Jesus chose to interact with others. Let's continue studying and we'll see some examples of that." We were looking at John 3:1–21, the conversation between Jesus and Nicodemus. First we noted that when Nicodemus sought out Jesus, the text says, "He came to Jesus at night" (John 3:2). "Tara, why do you think that Nicodemus came to Jesus at night?" I queried.

"Let's see," she said, thinking. "I remember something about this from a Bible study I did once. Wasn't it because he was a religious ruler, and to approach Jesus during the day would have caused quite a lot of political trouble for Nicodemus?"

"I think that's accurate," I responded. "We can glean something from Nicodemus's actions: timing. It's all in the timing. Nicodemus sought Jesus out when *it was best for him.* The same thing is true today. When someone is really ready to have a meaningful conversation—to share something significant in their life—they plan the time that is best for them. Like your kids, for example. Let's say you're busy preparing dinner and Junior comes in the back door, gives you a quick kiss on the cheek, and dashes up to his room while text-messaging his friends on his cell phone. That's probably not an opportune moment in which to have a significant conversation. However, let's say that after dinner, Junior approaches you just as you are about to sit down, turn on the TV, and see what's happening on your favorite show. He says something like, 'Hey, Mom, do you have a minute?' *That's* the opportune time for you to listen to your son.

"The second observation we make about meaningful conversation is in John 3:3 where Jesus says, 'I tell you the truth.' Jesus always tells truth. He doesn't pull out a story from His childhood so that He can better relate to the person's situation. He doesn't say, 'Oh, I know just how you feel!' when He most certainly did, since He is God, after all. Instead, He listens and then responds with truth. You can do the same thing. You see, what happens when we try to relate to someone by sharing something from our own past is that we inadvertently end up devaluing them by taking the attention off of their need. They came to you not to hear an anecdote from your past but to share what's on their mind. Jesus understood humankind and knew how important it is to *stay on track* with what is on the heart of the one sharing. We need to do likewise.

"Another way of unintentionally devaluing another is when we say, 'Oh! I know *just* how you feel!' The truth of the matter is that we *don't* know exactly how another person feels. To say that is to minimize the importance of their feelings. It's like saying, 'Oh, what you're going through is common, it's not unique, and therefore it's not important.'

"Actually, *none* of those statements are accurate. When a person, especially our own child, is going through something and has mustered up enough courage to approach us and to want to share what is on his or her mind, to minimize the situation is unthinkable. It's devaluing and disheartening. And yet, unknowingly, and perhaps with the best of intentions, we do just that, over and over again."

When I finished, Tara sat there with a thoughtful expression on her face. "I know I've done that, Ele. I so want to identify with my kids, to let them know I understand and care. As soon as I hear something with which I can identify, I'm off to the races, telling my story about me. But I'm beginning to see how Jesus would handle a conversation with my kids, and it's much different than what I've been doing!"

"Are you willing to go on and see what else is there in the text for us on this subject?" I questioned. "I know it's a lot to absorb in one setting."

"Don't stop," Tara responded. "I *want* to learn. Bring it on!"

"Jesus said to Nicodemus, 'No one can see the kingdom of God unless he is born again' (John 3:3). Nicodemus's response was, 'How can a man be born when he is old?' (John 3:4). It was clear to Jesus that Nicodemus didn't grasp what He was trying to teach him. Instead of putting Nicodemus down or arguing with him, Jesus listened to his response. Nicodemus's response gave Jesus insight about his level of understanding. This is exactly how to have a great conversation with your kids! Listen to how they respond. Listen to what they say. They are actually *gifting you with what they are thinking.* The more that we see conversation as a gift, as an opportunity to better understand another person, the more effective and the more like Jesus we will be in that other person's life. However, the opposite is also true. If we only listen to *how* something is said instead of *what* is being said, we shortchange our opportunity to come alongside of them and to partner with who the Holy Spirit is desiring to be in their lives! Or if we only listen long enough to hear something with which we disagree and then pounce on the sharer, you can bet that sharer will think twice before sharing with us again!

"We then see Jesus doing something very interesting with Nicodemus. When Jesus realizes that Nicodemus doesn't understand Him, that he isn't grasping the truth, Jesus takes him from the known to the unknown. He gives Nicodemus an example that Nicodemus can relate to and helps him cross over from the known—the truth in the illustration—to a deeper truth, the unknown (John 3:5–8). We, as parents, can do this very effectively with our kids. It's our responsibility to know our kids, to know what they're like. That way, when we need to help them understand something they're not able to grasp, we are able to think of who they are and give illustrations that will make a bridge for them to cross over, helping them to grasp the deeper insight. Does that make sense?"

"It sure does. I just hope I can remember all of this!" Tara replied.

"Well," I said, chuckling, "it's not going anywhere. It's all right there in John 3!" I continued, "The last thing we see Jesus do in this pivotal conversation with Nicodemus is that He restates the truth, leaving a challenge for Nicodemus. We see no manipulating, no cajoling, no guilt-tripping. Jesus clearly states truth and then challenges Nicodemus to 'live by the truth' (John 3:21). And Tara, we need to do the same with others. We need to do the same with our own kids. We must take them to Jesus, who is Truth. We challenge them and then we leave the rest to the Holy Spirit and to them. Remember, it's the *Holy Spirit's* job to convict, *not ours*! (John 16:8). Our joy is to share truth in a way in which the other person is able to receive it."

"Boy, I can hardly wait to have the chance to put this into practice!" exclaimed Tara. "The only thing is, I'll need to have my Bible open so that I can follow Jesus' example."

"Not a bad idea," I responded. "Not a bad idea at all."

10

Learning to be an active listener

I have had the worst week of my life!" Lynette exclaimed. She had caught my eye as I was walking into Starbucks to meet her. It was as if she couldn't wait to share. And I couldn't wait to hear. There would be no beverage order for me that day. I sat down, faced Lynette, and said, "Lynette, I'm so sorry to hear that—tell me about it."

"Well, my boss is coming into town on Tuesday and I need to plan and prepare a reception for her. I still need to complete last month's paperwork that is piling up on my desk. Clients are forming a line at my door, complaining about all sorts of dumb things!"

I had to bite my tongue so that I wouldn't interrupt Lynette's outburst. She was frustrated and she obviously needed to vent. At first it seemed that Lynette was struggling with an organizational issue. I could have ascertained that and then jumped in with some helpful ideas on how to accomplish her task and better manage her time, and then top it off with the phone number of a caterer to hire for the reception.

But Lynette wasn't done sharing . . . not nearly so. After taking a quick sip of her drink, Lynette continued. "And that's not all. My sister called me at three o'clock this morning. She was supposed to be in Texas at a conference, but she decided to leave the conference early. She got a late flight out of Dallas and when she landed here she was stinking drunk. She really likes those little bottles that you can buy on flights. She and her seatmate must have had quite a party on that flight."

Here was another chance for me to jump in. I could have sympathized with her over her sister's poor choice and how rude it was to wake her up, especially on a work night. But I waited. There was more that Lynette wanted to share.

"She called me from her cell phone. She sounded okay and she said that she was going to hang out with a guy she met on the plane. But then her phone went dead. I guess the battery was low." Lynette paused. "So I've been sitting by the phone since three waiting to hear from my sister." Another pause. "I'm really worried about her. She drinks too much and sleeps around too much, and I don't know how to help her."

There it is—the root issue. Did you hear it? Lynette was saying, "What is my role in my sister's life?" If I had prematurely interrupted the conversation by interjecting my own experiences, I would have missed it. If I had volunteered my opinion on her job or her sister, I wouldn't have heard the real issue. If I had said, "Oh, the same thing happened to me when I was your age," just look at what would have been missed!

Spiritual mentor, it's been my experience that active listening is a learned skill, not something that comes naturally to most of us. Most of us have been on the receiving end of what it feels like to try to share with someone, only to be cut off by the other person's good intentions of sharing a similar experience. Since this aspect of active listening is so essential to being an effective spiritual mentor, let's pause and look at this concept in a bit of detail.

Active listening is a big part of the "how" of being a valuable spiritual mentor to your mentees. To help focus our understanding on how to be an active listener, let's define what it means. *An active listener is one who intently listens to another person with the goal of being able to identify with the life of the one sharing in order to be a more effective tool in the hands of the Holy Spirit in the other person's life.* In order to further clarify this point, allow me to state what active listening is *not*. Active listening is not intently listening to the other person with the goal of being able to identify with the life of the one sharing in order to *interject personal life history* with the thought of *changing or manipulating* that person.

Spiritual mentoring is not the forum in which we share our stories, our opinions, and our "wisdom." Somehow this concept has gotten out there, and we have bought the lie that talking, sharing our life stories, and offering advice is what it means to spiritually mentor someone. I can assure you that is *not* spiritual mentoring. That is dumping on another person. That is puffing ourselves up. That is imposing on someone else. That is not being a spiritual mentor.

Just think about it for a minute. If that *were* what we were to do, wouldn't Scripture teach us that? Wouldn't the conversations that Jesus was a part of reflect that philosophy? Wouldn't there be illustration after illustration of how we are to share our life experiences with others? How would Philippians 2:1–2 be written? Perhaps something like this: "If you have any encouragement from identifying with me, if any comfort from hearing about my life, if any fellowship with my experience, if any advice and helpful comments, then make my joy complete by thinking like I think, having the same opinions, being one in experience and outcome." Obviously this is *not* what the Holy Word of God states.

What it does state is the following: "If you have any encouragement from being united *with Christ*, if any comfort from *his love*, if any fellowship with *the Spirit*, if any tenderness and compassion, then make my joy complete by being like-minded, having the same love, being one in spirit and purpose" (Philippians 2:1–2, italics added). Paul goes on to say, "Do nothing out of selfish ambition or vain conceit, but in humility consider others better than yourselves. Each of you should look not only to your own interests, but also to the interests of others" (Philippians 2:3–4).

The "working clothes," the "how" to "do nothing out of selfish ambition or vain conceit," but to "look not only to your own interests, but also to the interests of others" is to actively listen.

Our objective as spiritual mentors is to come alongside of another, partnering with who the Holy Spirit is being in her life by infusing truth into her reality . . . period. The focus is to always remain on Jesus, *not* on us. We are to take the other person to Jesus, to make her independently dependent on Him. They are to become followers of Jesus, not followers of us.

Active listening helps us be effective junior partners to the Holy Spirit. How? By not short-circuiting who the Spirit is being in the lives of others. When we say, "Oh, I know just how you feel," we short-circuit the Holy Spirit in their lives. Why? Because we are assuming the role of someone far greater than ourselves. We are usurping the position of the Holy Spirit! Only the Holy Spirit knows *exactly* how one feels. We may have very good intentions in saying that we know. But we don't know. We are unable to know. Only God knows and we must partner with Him for the good of the mentee and the glory of God.

Also, when we exclaim, "Oh, the *same thing* happened to me!" we are inadvertently devaluing that person's life experience. The Holy Spirit has allowed certain things to happen to them for a reason. That reason is so that they would choose to depend on Him, choose to think His thoughts, and decide to adjust their life patterns to reflect the Spirit's life pattern for them.

When we say, "I know just what you ought to do," we are implanting ourselves in place of who the Spirit is wanting to be in their lives. Perhaps without realizing it, we are becoming their "holy spirit." We are taking the place in their lives that only the Holy Spirit of God has a right to take. We as spiritual mentors must be very, very careful that we are only the "friend who attends the bridegroom" and not the "bridegroom" Himself, as stated in John 3:29. To put it bluntly, "He *must* become greater; I *must* become less" (John 3:30, italics added).

Being a spiritual mentor is serious stuff! It's not flitting into a room full of other women gathered around round tables. It's not viewing a DVD together and then breaking into groups to talk about it. It's not going on a weekend retreat and sharing morning devotions. It's so much more, so much deeper, so much more effective, and so much more honoring to God. It is partnering with the Holy Spirit in the life of another person. And *that* is amazing.

But there is responsibility in the call. And becoming an active listener is a very useful, very helpful tool to employ when mentoring another.

After allowing the person who is sharing to thoroughly "empty out" without making any comments in response, the active listener further enhances what the Holy Spirit desires to accomplish in the sharer's life by asking insightful questions. Insightful questions are questions that help the sharer better understand herself or the situation. Insightful questions are not to be used to gather unnecessary information for ourselves about the mentee. At times there is a fine line between the two, but the motivation of asking the question should be to clarify what the person has said, not to satisfy your own curiosity.

I'd like to give you a list of clarifying questions that you may want to memorize. These are open-ended questions that will help you as you partner with the Holy Spirit in the lives of your mentees.

- ❖ "Would you like to tell me more?" (This is always good to ask before making the assumption that the mentee is finished sharing.)
- ❖ "How does [fill-in-the-blank] make you feel?" (Succinctly restate what you thought you just heard.)
- ❖ "What are your options in this situation?"
- ❖ "How do you find yourself praying about this?"
- ❖ "What do you think Jesus is trying to teach you through this?"
- ❖ "How can you glorify God in this situation?" (This, by far, is a very valuable question to ask. It takes away the "why" of the situation and replaces it with a "how." This is exactly what the Holy Spirit would like us to choose to do.)

And conversely, here is a list of some ineffective comments to avoid:

- ❖ "I know just how you feel."
- ❖ "The same thing happened to me."
- ❖ "That's nothing! Let me tell you my story."
- ❖ "You have nothing to complain about."
- ❖ "You think that's something? Just you wait!"
- ❖ "Been there . . . done that."

It's good to remember the reasoning behind why we're spiritual mentors. We're spiritual mentors because we want to partner with who the Holy Spirit is being in the life of another person. We're spiritual mentors because we want to take someone else to Jesus and stay there with her. We're spiritual mentors in order to infuse truth into another's reality. We're spiritual mentors to be a human bridge over which another person on the journey may cross from life to deep life in Jesus. And in order to help us accomplish our purpose, we must learn to use the very effective tool of active listening.

11

Megan

egan is a perky, "with it" type of young mom. Her short, curly black hair is fixed in a style that accentuates her dark eyes. Her clothes are expertly chosen to show off the attractive figure she has, even after bearing four children. Those same four children are well behaved and get good grades in school. Her parents are still together after forty-some years. Megan's brother and sister both are married to their original spouses—a rarity in today's society. She works part-time only because she wants to. Her husband, Tom, makes more than enough for their comfortable lifestyle. Their home is tastefully furnished, and the backyard is complete with a tree house, swing set, and built-in grill. Megan is living a life that most people would envy.

The only thing is, Megan isn't in love with her husband. Granted, she loves and appreciates qualities *about* her husband. Tom is nice, is faithful, and is good with at least the two kids who are like him. He is nice to Megan and denies her nothing. So it's a fairy-tale life except one annoying fact: Megan's in love with someone else. Tom just "doesn't do it" for Megan. He never did.

Megan knew as she was walking down the aisle at her wedding that the marriage was a mistake. But Tom had met every point on her "husband wish list." He is handsome, a good provider financially, sexually faithful, a believer in Jesus, comes from a good family, and her parents really like him. But there's the rub. Her *parents*—not Megan —really like him.

When Megan was in high school, she met Mark. Mark was two years older than she was. He was a weight lifter and he worked as a lifeguard at the local pool. Mark had a great body; that was evident to anyone. During high school Megan and Mark only knew each other because their families both went to the same church. After high school Mark moved to another state to attend a Christian university. Two years later Megan decided to attend that same university. There, in that context, Mark and Megan started dating.

Their relationship was fulfilling, at least to Megan. They studied together, they had meals together, and they attended school functions together . . . always together. On some nights, instead of going out on a date, Mark would pull out his guitar and sing to Megan. The two of them would find themselves laughing, falling back on his dorm bed. Their conversations were deep. They challenged one another about biblical concepts, debated over questionable passages, and discussed the nuances of Greek words. They were falling in love with one another.

To this day Megan still isn't sure what happened. One day she received a short letter from Mark. He wrote that he felt their relationship was moving too quickly. He decided that they should stop seeing each other for a while. He just broke it off with her cold turkey. Megan was devastated. She had no idea what she had done to cause him to not love her anymore. She would have done anything to get Mark back. But Mark had somehow moved on. He was over her.

Mark transferred to another university not long after he wrote the letter to Megan. He was just gone. Megan was left with a deeply broken heart. A few months later, Tom entered Megan's life. Tom was stable, he was patient with her, he wasn't pushy, and he didn't pry into her past. After a few months, Tom and Megan were a steady couple. One weekend they drove back to Megan's home for Tom to meet her mom and dad. The two of them immediately gushed over Tom. "Oh, he's so solid," they declared. "What a good provider he'd be! He's down to earth, sensible, and so smart." When Tom asked Megan to marry him, she could think of no good reason not to do so. So she numbly went through the motions of a bridal shower, of planning the details of the ceremony (which her mom and sister did most of), and dutifully tried on wedding dress after wedding dress until her sister exclaimed with pleasure, "Oh! *That's* the one!" Megan purchased the dress her sister chose and tucked it away in the back of her closet.

The day of their wedding arrived. Megan's mom found her sitting all alone in her childhood room, going through a little box that contained reminders of Mark: ticket stubs to the county fair, a menu from "their" restaurant, a guitar pick that he had left in her car . . . the little things that made them *them*. Megan's mom was mortified. "How dare you be thinking of that boy when you're about to marry such a fine man as Tom!" her mother scolded. "What in the world do you think you're doing? You're about to become Tom's wife! We're going to get rid of all this baggage once and for all!" Megan's mother then took the small box out in the backyard, placed it in the grill, and lit a match to it. Megan's mementos of Mark caught fire and then quickly turned to ashes. They were gone.

That was nearly twelve years ago. In reality, Mark never left Megan's heart or thoughts. She thinks about what it would be like to be married to Mark, what their children would look like, how they would hold each other. She hears the laughter that would ring from their hearts as they enjoyed life together. Then she forces herself to return and live another day in her reality: Tom . . . reliable, dependable, boring Tom. Megan loves their children. They're great kids. The third one, the one most like Tom, annoys her with his whining, his logic, his "nerdiness." "He's so much like his father," others comment. Megan agrees. They're both nerdy.

Her in-laws are all right. They come for a mandatory holiday visit each year so that they can see their grandkids. Tom and his folks don't converse much, so Megan feels the responsibility and pressure of keeping up the conversation during the short visits. She's always exhausted by the time her in-laws finally leave.

Her parents have been pleased with her marriage to Tom over the years. All that they predicted has come true. Tom is a good provider. He is solid. He has done well for himself and his family. Their anxiety over Megan's future has been neatly and tidily put to rest. Megan tries to hide her resentment toward her mother for being so controlling, for only thinking of herself, for helping to mess up her life. Megan attempts to make the best of the fact that this is her life and she needs to live it just as it is. She manages to control herself, at least for another day, from screaming out at the top of her voice, "Doesn't anyone get it? This isn't the life I was supposed to live! This isn't the man I was destined to marry! I'm in love with another man and I'll never know the joy of waking up in his arms, of building on our mutual dreams together, of growing old next to the one I love! Don't you see? Don't you understand?"

My heart cries with Megan's heart. Her loss is tremendous; her grief unvoiced. The weight of her loss is almost suffocating her. She is desperate. She is a follower of Jesus, and she wants, more than anything, to be like Jesus. But she feels so trapped . . . so unfulfilled . . . that she can barely breathe.

Let's fast-forward to my divine encounter with Megan—at a spring luncheon for the women in our church. She was there with three friends she had brought from her neighborhood. Their table needed a fourth person, so they invited me to join them. During the course of the event, we chatted about family, jobs, other seasonal events, the church . . . all the usual topics that comprise small talk. I could tell there was more to Megan than what she was allowing us to see around that table. There was quality. There was passion. There was depth. I was intrigued by her. So, when I received a phone call from her a few days later and she asked if we could get together and talk, I responded with an enthusiastic yes!

We met at a coffee shop in a nearby mall. It smelled homey and inviting, and we each had a hot beverage in our hands as we slipped into a corner booth. After the usual pleasantries shared at the beginning of any conversation, I leaned in toward Megan and gently asked, "Why are we here?" The tears almost instantly surfaced. It took a few moments for Megan to regain her composure. After dabbing her dark eyes with a napkin, she began opening her heart to me. Twelve years of regret, disappointment, guilt, anger, resentment, and hopelessness came pouring out. I listened, not moving a muscle, not wanting to take anything away from what Megan was sharing. She was a woman in deep pain. She was a follower of Jesus who was in desperation. She was entrusting me with her deepest, darkest secret: she wasn't in love with her husband.

Where does one begin to help mend such a broken heart? What verse in God's Word would be an appropriate bandage to put over such a gaping wound? What prayer could be said to soothe such grief, to miraculously make Megan love Tom? Insulting Megan with such trivial solutions, belittling her pain with such superficiality, or betraying her trust with a pat answer was unthinkable.

What happened next? Hope was offered. How? In the form of truth. With the Holy Spirit guiding me, I offered truth to Megan. What was the Holy Spirit doing in Megan's life? He was purposefully and deliberately utilizing her life circumstances to gently, but consistently, make her more like Him. Only she couldn't see it for the pain. As we talked I challenged her, as I do with all the women I mentor, to answer a basic question. "What do you want? Are you looking for a quick fix or do you want your life transformed by Jesus Himself?" Megan opted for the life transformation. Yes, she wanted some relief, some perspective. But more than that, Megan wanted the authentic Jesus.

We began to meet, going to the gospel of John as our reference. "In the beginning . . ." I love how the Holy Spirit chose to begin this account of how Jesus lived when He was on earth. Beginning . . . who among us doesn't want a new beginning at one time or another in our lives? That's *exactly* what Jesus offers each of us. He's *in* the beginning. He *is* the beginning no matter where we each are in our personal life stories. He offered a new beginning to Megan that day.

Megan and I have met for nearly two years. Each time we meet we are both amazed how the Holy Spirit has taken us to just the right passage in John. It's uncanny. I see this over and over again with each woman I spiritually mentor. The Holy Spirit loves the fact that *He* is their Teacher, that *He* is their Counselor. We go to the Word of God to see what it has to say about transforming us, rather than running to this or that verse using it as a spiritual aspirin. You see, God desires to transform us—to change us to become like Jesus. He's really not in the business of "fixing" us. In fact, God uses our life situations and circumstances in order to help make us more like Jesus. What a thought that is! You may ask, "You mean it *isn't* all about *me*? Life and all it holds is actually opportunity after opportunity to become more like Jesus? Wahoo!"

God heard Megan's cries for help. He is honoring her desire to "be" Jesus in her marriage. He is giving her strength, perspective, and grace in daily measures. As we go to the Word of God together, He is constantly giving her insight upon insight, and, as a result, she is growing up in Him. For example, in John 1:35–42, we see two disciples deciding to follow Jesus. "Turning around, Jesus saw them following and asked, 'What do you want?'" (John 1:38). That is a great question for a follower of Jesus. And that's a great question for Megan. So I asked her, "Megan, what do you want from Jesus?" That question alone helped Megan pour out expectations that she had about Jesus, about what it meant to be a follower of Jesus, about how disappointed she was in Him, about how angry she was that He didn't do something about Mark, and about how He seemingly let her down and tricked her. It allowed the Holy Spirit to deal with some core issues that were blocking spiritual growth in Megan's life. It lifted invisible burdens that she had been carrying, alone, for years. Truth is in the process of setting Megan free.

Another example of how the Holy Spirit used God's Word to grow Megan up in Himself came from John 5:6. Jesus asked the man who had been sick for thirty-eight years, "Do you want to get well?" (John 5:6). Again, I asked Megan the question, "Megan, do *you* want to get well?" Her answer to this question is also helping to set her free.

Both of those deep, probing questions are also questions that the Holy Spirit wants *us* to answer, just as Megan did. Megan chose to deal with her issues, to take the time and effort to answer the questions honestly and deeply, and the Holy Spirit was quick to apply grace and truth to her bravery.

Tom hasn't changed. Megan has. She is being "transformed by the renewing of [her] mind" (Romans 12:2) as the Word of God is being correctly applied to her life by the Holy Spirit. She is being freed as truth is infused into her reality. She notices the giving, the caring, the patience, and the kindness that Tom lavishes on her. She is able to think less about Mark and to focus more emotional energy on her children as well as on Tom. She is growing up in Jesus. Megan is realizing the opportunity God has given her for spiritual growth. One truth in her reality is that she may never be entirely fulfilled being married to Tom. But that would also be part of her reality if she had been married to Mark, as well. This life isn't about being personally fulfilled; it's about becoming more and more like Jesus *through*, *in*, and *in spite of* the particular circumstances that life may afford us. As Megan understands and lives out truth in her reality, she is seeing growth and change in *her* that is having an effect on those around her.

"Wahoo," indeed!

12

Standing firm with you

There are certain phrases in the Word of God that the Spirit high-lights when it comes to spiritually mentoring another person. One such phrase is "stand firm." Most of us are familiar with the importance that this phrase has in the New Testament. Peter reminds us that our enemy is "like a roaring lion," and what the follower of Jesus is instructed to do when the Devil comes around is to "stand firm" (1 Peter 5:8–9). However, it's good for us to realize that the concept of "standing firm" is seen throughout all of the written Word of God, starting in Exodus 14:13.

In this passage, the Israelites had just left Egypt, beginning their march to the land God had promised to them. Anxiety and fear were thick in the air as those just-freed slaves took their first steps of freedom. Moses was leading the people away from Egypt, but Pharaoh and his vast army were close behind. "Then the Lord said to Moses, 'Tell the Israelites to turn back and . . . encamp by the sea. . . . Pharaoh will think, "The Israelites are wandering around the land in confusion, hemmed in by the desert"'" (Exodus 14:1–3). That was an interesting game plan, especially from the perspective of the Israelites. But God had something greater in mind than their immediate level of stress.

The passage goes on to read, "I will gain glory for myself through Pharaoh and all his army, and the Egyptians will know that I am the Lord" (Exodus 14:4). God had another level of reality that He was promoting—His reality. So Moses did as the Lord instructed him, and this is how the people responded:

> As Pharaoh approached, the Israelites looked up, and there were the Egyptians, marching after them. They were terrified and cried out to the Lord. They said to Moses, "Was it because there were no graves in Egypt that you brought us to the desert to die? What have you done to us by bringing us out of Egypt? Didn't we say to you in Egypt, 'Leave us alone; let us serve the Egyptians'? It would have been better for us to serve the Egyptians than to die in the desert!" Moses answered the people, "Do not be afraid. Stand firm and you will see the deliverance the Lord will bring you today. The Egyptians you see today you will never see again. The Lord will fight for you; you need only to be still." (Exodus 14:10–14)

There's some great truth in that reality. First of all, we see newly freed slaves beginning their walk with God. They had to have been excited and nervous about their newfound freedom. Up to this point in their lives, they had always been under the control of other people. They were used to reacting, not initiating. All was new. And then they met their first test: the enemy was after them. They could smell and feel the breath of the enemy on their necks; they could hear the snarl in the enemy's voice; they were frozen with fear.

Do you see the application to spiritual mentoring? The women you will be mentoring have been slaves to something in their lives. They will come to you because they want to grow in Jesus. They will come to you because they see something in your life that they desire. They also will come to you for help. There's an enemy in their lives to whom they have been enslaved. They want freedom. As you partner with who the Holy Spirit is being in their lives, the enemy will become apparent. Your task as a spiritual mentor will be to infuse the truth of Scripture into that reality. What this will do is give them options that they did not have before. When they choose to leave their tormentors, to break free from the enemy, there will be great rejoicing, but they will also need to realize that they have other choices to make as well. When the first test of their newfound freedom comes up, the mentee will have a choice about what to do: react as usual by going back into the bad situation, or initiate a new response based on the truth we have inserted into their reality. What is that truth? To "stand firm and [they] will see the deliverance the Lord will bring" (Exodus 14:13).

The strategy to "stand firm" is seen other places in Scripture as well.

❖ 2 Chronicles 20:17—"You will not have to fight this battle. Take up your positions; stand firm and see the deliverance the Lord will give you."

❖ Proverbs 12:7—"Wicked people are overthrown and are no more, but the house of the righteous stands firm."

❖ Isaiah 7:9—"If you do not stand firm in your faith, you will not stand at all."

❖ Matthew 10:22—"He who stands firm to the end will be saved."

❖ Luke 21:19—"By standing firm you will gain life."

❖ 1 Corinthians 15:58—"Therefore, my dear brothers, stand firm. Let nothing move you. Always give yourselves fully to the work of the Lord, because you know that your labor in the Lord is not in vain."

❖ 1 Corinthians 16:13—"Be on your guard; stand firm in the faith; be men of courage; be strong."

❖ Galatians 5:1—"It is for freedom that Christ has set us free. Stand firm, then, and do not let yourselves be burdened again by a yoke of slavery."

❖ Ephesians 6:13–18—"Therefore put on the full armor of God, so that when the day of evil comes, you may be able to stand your ground, and after you have done everything, to stand. Stand firm, then, with the belt of truth buckled around your waist, with the breastplate of righteousness in place, and with your feet fitted with the readiness that comes from the gospel of peace. In addition to all this, take up the shield of faith, with which you can extinguish all the flaming arrows of the evil one. Take the helmet of salvation and the sword of the Spirit, which is the word of God. And pray in the Spirit on all occasions with all kinds of prayers and requests. With this in mind, be alert and always keep on praying for all the saints."

- ❖ 2 Thessalonians 2:15—"So then, brothers, stand firm and hold to the teachings we passed on to you, whether by word of mouth or by letter."
- ❖ 2 Timothy 2:19—"Nevertheless, God's solid foundation stands firm, sealed with this inscription: 'The Lord knows those who are his,' and, 'Everyone who confesses the name of the Lord must turn away from wickedness.'"
- ❖ James 5:8—"You, too, be patient and stand firm, because the Lord's coming is near."
- ❖ 1 Peter 5:8–9—"Be self-controlled and alert. Your enemy the devil prowls around like a roaring lion looking for someone to devour. Resist him, standing firm in the faith, because you know that your brothers throughout the world are undergoing the same kind of sufferings."

As we read the above passages, it is easy to get excited about "standing firm." The outcome of standing firm is impressive: the Lord will deliver, we will be saved, we gain life, our labor in the Lord is not in vain, we'll be people of faith, and we'll be strong. However, the actual stance of "standing firm" is exhausting!

Just picture it: You are in a precarious situation, at best. It's a known situation, one you have found yourself in many times before. Each time this situation comes up in your life, you have great intentions of doing something different that will cause a healthier outcome. You can feel your body tensing; you can hear the words forming in your mind. This time, you're going to say something brilliant that will disarm the situation. You're going to walk through it with dignity and calmness. But when the moment comes, you end up reacting the same as always, spewing out the same hurtful, damaging words, shaking your fist in the air, and leaving the situation feeling defeated . . . just as before.

How do we apply this spiritual truth to our reality? We know what our reality is; we live it every day, and the damage that defeat after defeat causes is taking its toll on us. So, we go to the Word of God and find that we are to "stand firm." So what? To "stand firm" seems so passive, so nonengaged, so useless. But in reality, standing firm is one of the most exhausting, courageous positions of battle. It is much easier to pump yourself up, let out a shrilling war whoop, raise the spear above your head, and run head-on into battle. The adrenaline rush is a supercharge, and the mere flurry of activity convinces you that something good must be happening. But to stand firm . . . to not move . . . to be unwavering as the Enemy is rushing toward you with his spear aimed at your heart? It takes every ounce of energy you can muster. It takes an overwhelming confidence in the One who has given the command to "stand firm." It takes faith. It takes truth. It takes self-control.

Perhaps the following email conversation between one of my mentees and me will help to flesh out this concept of "standing firm."

Dear Morgan,

I'm just writing you a quick email to see how you are this morning. You have committed yourself to growth, to change, and to Jesus. You are partnering with the Holy Spirit as He now has greater access to your soul and spirit. May you be encouraged in your deepest inner person. Remember, "[You] are God's workmanship, created in Christ Jesus to do good works, which God prepared in advance for [you] to do" (Ephesians 2:10).

Surround your mind with truth. The battle takes place in the mind, as Romans 8:5–9 reminds us:

Those who live according to the sinful nature have their minds set on what that nature desires; but those who live in accordance with the Spirit have their minds set on what the Spirit desires. The mind of sinful man is death, but the mind controlled by the Spirit is life and peace; the sinful mind is hostile to God. It does not submit to God's law, nor can it do so. Those controlled by the sinful nature cannot please God. You, however, are controlled not by the sinful nature but by the Spirit, if the Spirit of God lives in you.

We are instructed to set our minds on what the Spirit desires, which is life and peace. May you be a pursuer of life and peace as you walk in His footsteps today.

Standing firm with you,
Ele

Dear Ele,

Thank you so much! All I can say is, "God is great!"

I am calm and peaceful and can feel the Holy Spirit working. My husband is hurt and trying not to act like it, but I can see it. We had some "us" time this morning and I was able to remember God in everything . . . so far so good. I called two friends and my sister and told them about our blessings yesterday and asked them to keep my husband, our family, and me in their prayers.

Thank you for your reminder and encouragement to stand firm. I love it and need it. Consistency—that is the word of the year for me!

I love you and praise God that our lives have crossed. Thank you for walking God's walk. You are the example I have been praying for.

Now I understand the closing to your email, because I, too, am standing firm in Him, with Him!

Morgan

Standing firm with you

As I was writing this chapter, I received another email from Morgan.

Dear Ele,

I don't want to be unhappily married anymore. I don't want to inflict any more damage on my children.

I asked Greg if he would seek help with me. His response was that it hasn't worked in the past, that going to church and Bible study aren't working for him now, and that he'll think about it. (That basically means no.)

I tried to keep my cool . . . but I didn't. The conversation went south and I yelled at him. I told him he had to go to counseling with me or I'm leaving. I know, that was the wrong thing to say! And by the way, I also told him not to come home after work.

I feel hopeless. I'm trying to seek God's truth, but it's not working and I'm afraid I'm going to lose it with my kids. Not physically, of course, but I don't want to be short with Britney or yell at her.

I know you are in the middle of this project and I am so sorry to be bothering you. But I will do whatever you say. And if you need to direct me to someone else until you get back . . . well, I don't want to, but I'll understand.

Thank you, Ele!

Morgan

Do you feel her pain? Do you sense her disappointment, frustration, and hopelessness? How would you help Morgan to stand firm in this situation? What would you say? What would you do? I'll share with you what I did. The first thing I did was to pray for her, that she would have the strength and perspective not to do anything stupid. The next thing I did was to pray for myself, that God would grant me the help that Morgan was reaching out for.

After that, I called her. I asked her if she wanted to share her story with me, and she did. She talked for a long time about what had happened and how it was like or unlike their typical cycle of relating to each other. I have found that it is helpful for women to stand firm if they can determine their "emotional cycles" within their relationships. First, they figure out what triggers the cycle, such as an attitude, a tone of voice, or a time of the month. Then you can help them ascertain what the middle of the cycle typically looks like. Finally, discuss what marks the end of their cycle.

After we talked through where Morgan and Greg were in their emotional cycle, I offered her a way to continue to stand firm in her marriage. She desires a good marriage. She wants it to work with Greg. So I told her that while she knows what Greg is not willing to do, she needs to find out what he would be willing to do in order to strengthen their marriage. I gave Morgan some "homework" to do, as well. Answering these questions will help her as she strives to stand firm, and they will help me as I attempt to infuse truth into her reality.

- ❖ Write down the things you are most angry and disappointed about in your life. Is it Greg? Is it yourself? Is it God? What is it?
- ❖ Write down five of the reasons that you married Greg in the first place.
- ❖ Which of those reasons are indicative of your reality now with Greg?
- ❖ What are three things that you can do, right now, to help this situation?

I then prayed with and for her, asking the Holy Spirit not to waste this situation but to use it to help Morgan become more like Jesus. We prayed that the Holy Spirit would recleanse their home and send strong angels to stand guard over all of them. We asked that the Holy Spirit would also be working in Greg's life and that Morgan and Greg would be able to experience peace and joy in their relationship.

I then told Morgan to call me if she needed me and told her that I loved her and believed in her. My last words to her were, "Keep standing firm in truth." I could sense her smile of relief over the phone and the renewed determination that accompanied that smile.

That is what it means to stand firm: continuing to be who the Lord desires one to be, in spite of changing circumstances. It is actively listening to another, helping her recognize truth in her reality. It is to consistently pray for her and with her. Stand firm, dear spiritual mentor. Stand firm.

13

Brandi

Beautiful. Together. Challenging. Aloof. Those are some of the words that I would use to describe Brandi if asked. Her hair is always smartly styled, her Arbonne cosmetics are consistently on "just so," and her clothes are stylish without being extreme. She arrives early to engagements, even though she has four little ones. Brandi is one of those ladies everyone depends on without anyone saying so. She is stable and steady; she's there for others. Brandi is a good person to have as a friend. She's low maintenance and self-contained. None of this comes as a surprise, for, you see, Brandi is a pastor's wife.

Brandi and I have known each other for years. Well, better said, we have known *of* one another for several years. We see each other at conferences, bump into one another at workshops, and I hear of her and her husband through mutual acquaintances. I like Brandi. She's a sharp woman. She's articulate, well studied, and a good conversationalist. She's one of those women I seek out whenever I know we may be attending the same convention. The age difference between us is a nonissue, for Brandi is an "old soul." She views life and what it brings to her with thoughtfulness, integrity, and faith.

When I received the phone call from Brandi, I was pleased and a bit honored. Perhaps she wanted me to come and speak at her church. Maybe she was asking if we could co-lead a seminar. So when she asked if I could set aside some time to spiritually mentor her, I was taken back a bit. "Me mentor Brandi?" I thought. "Why, *she* mentors *others*! What could I offer Brandi that she doesn't already know?" As standard procedure, we decided that we would both pray about the situation for a week. She hung up the phone and I began talking to the Lord. "Lord, what do I have to offer Brandi?" I queried. No immediate answer was revealed to me. It was a good thing that we had committed to praying about this for a week. I needed the entire week to get direction from the Lord about Brandi.

In my own daily intake of God's Word, I was reading through Galatians, one of the letters that Paul wrote to the first generation of believers. They were going through spiritual growing pains and needed some encouragement to keep their faith pure and strong in Jesus alone. That sounded good to me as well! So I was reading along and came to the part of the letter that said, "Carry each other's burdens" (Galatians 6:2). A little later Paul reminds the reader, "As we have opportunity, let us do good to all people, especially to those who belong to the family of believers" (Galatians 6:10).

After reading those verses I prayed, "Lord, are You talking to me about Brandi? Does she need my help? How can I come alongside of her and partner with who You are in her life? How can I 'do good' to her?" I then knew that I needed to begin meeting with Brandi.

During our phone conversation, Brandi's voice sounded relieved when she realized that we would be meeting regularly by email or by phone. Yes, it's a little different way to spiritually mentor someone, but it works for other types of relationships, so I figured it would for this one as well. I asked her to please dedicate a notebook to our time together and to also begin reading for herself in John, the book of beginnings. She was willing and ready to do so.

Our times together in John were enriching for both of us. Brandi was a quick learner and applied her sharp mind to what Jesus was saying, as well as what He refrained from saying. It was an "iron sharpening iron" type of relationship. I was pleased to be invited into Brandi's life but really didn't know why I was there. She didn't have a lot of things to "fix," not that I was in the business of fixing others. It's just that as one commits to allowing the Holy Spirit to enter and be Teacher and Counselor in one's life, one assumes that He will do a lot of rearranging in the life as a result. Brandi's life seemed pretty much intact and ordered . . . until we came to John 11.

As is my usual custom, I asked Brandi to read out loud. She began reading the account of Mary, Martha, and their brother, Lazarus. It was a familiar passage of what happened to this family when they ran into deep stress. Lazarus became very sick. "So the sisters sent word to Jesus, 'Lord, the one you love is sick.' When he heard this, Jesus said, 'This sickness will not end in death. No, it is for God's glory so that God's Son may be glorified through it.' Jesus loved Martha and her sister and Lazarus. Yet when he heard that Lazarus was sick, he stayed where he was two more days" (John 11:3–6). Brandi stopped reading. "Oh, Brandi, please read on," I coached her. I heard nothing but silence . . . not one word. "Hello, Brandi?" I said, thinking that we were cut off. "Brandi?" I repeated. After another silent pause, I heard her breathing. It was that hard, heavy, increased-pace breathing, the kind that is used when one is attempting to impede the flow of tears. Brandi was crying.

The Spirit stopped me from saying anything to Brandi. Instead I turned my thoughts to God directly. "Oh, Jesus," I prayed, "thank You for being with Your daughter Brandi right now. Thank You that You love her and that what is going on in her will be used for Your glory and her good. Help us together, Jesus." And then I waited in silence.

The crying was the kind that flows from a broken heart, from dreams that would never be realized, from moments that would not be shared with the one for whom they were intended. I prayed as I waited, until I felt released by the Spirit to inquire, "Do you want to talk about it?"

I could sense the hesitation in Brandi. Her crying, now a soft weeping, was caught up short by the question. I could feel her struggle, so I prayed as I waited. If this was the time and moment to share, I prayed that she would be able to do so. If this was not of the Lord, I prayed that

Brandi would have the wisdom to quietly decline the invitation. I heard her clear her voice and then she began to haltingly share her story.

Shortly after they were married, Brandi discovered that her husband was staying up late on his computer. She assumed that he was working on his sermon or that he was emailing a seminary friend. The late computer nights became a norm and Brandi resigned herself to "supporting her husband" by falling asleep night after night alone in their bed. Brandi confessed that she felt left out and devalued by the late-night computer usage but also felt guilty for her feelings, thinking she was being selfish with her husband.

One night, a few years into this habit, Brandi woke up around two o'clock in the morning feeling sick to her stomach. She dragged herself out of bed, passed the kids' rooms, and went down the stairs to her husband's basement office. She was going to let him know that he should probably sleep in the guest bedroom since she was starting to feel so ill. As she quietly entered the office, what met her eyes only made her feel sicker than she already was. There was her husband, deeply engaged in watching pornography on the Internet. He was so engrossed in it that it took him a minute or two to realize that he was not alone. Their eyes met and he knew that she knew. His only response was, "What are you doing here? Get out! This is my space and my time. You have no right to be here!"

Brandi was shocked, sickened, and dismayed. She turned and slowly dragged her weak body back up the stairs. She tried to go back to bed but passed most of the rest of that night kneeling over the toilet as she cried and vomited, the pain in her heart overshadowing the ache in her body. The flu ran its course not only through Brandi's body but also through her entire family. She used the sickness as an excuse to stay away from extended family and friends. Her heart was broken and no one could mend it. Gene, the one who should have helped her, was a burden and drain to her. He was angry and sullen toward her, keeping his distance from Brandi and the family. She was truly all alone and she felt entirely abandoned.

As well as feeling abandoned, Brandi also felt trapped. What was she to do? To whom would she go for help? Since Gene was the senior pastor of the church, she felt that she did not have the emotional infrastructure to deal with the unbearable pain she was carrying. She also felt very disappointed in Jesus. Jesus had always been there for her. As a young child, Brandi had learned to talk to Jesus and had learned to hear His voice above the din of others. She loved to spend hours with Him in prayer and meditation. She knew the importance of taking everything to Jesus, which Gene and she had done before and after their marriage; at least she thought they had. She felt so very betrayed by Gene . . . and, in the depth of her being, she felt betrayed by Jesus as well.

One of Brandi's favorite people in the Bible was Mary, the sister of Martha and Lazarus. Brandi identified with Mary. Brandi, as well, would have "poured perfume on the Lord and wiped his feet with her hair" (John 11:2). She, too, would have "chosen what is better" if she had been with Jesus in the home of Mary and Martha (Luke 10:42). And now, on the phone call, Brandi was sharing in Mary's words when Mary sent word to Jesus, "Lord, the one you love is sick" (John 11:3).

How appropriate . . . how specific . . . how kind of the Spirit to take Brandi to these words at this moment in her life—the very words that Mary had sent to Jesus. "Lord, the one you love is sick." Yes, Gene was sick. He was very, very sick.

The next part of the account in John brought more tears to Brandi's heart: "When he heard this, Jesus said, 'This sickness will not end in death. No, *it is for God's glory so that God's Son may be glorified through it'*" (John 11:4, italics added). Was it possible, Lord? Was it possible to bring glory to Jesus through this horrible "sickness" that Gene had?

Brandi mustered her emotional strength and read on. "Jesus loved Martha and her sister *and Lazarus*. Yet when he heard that Lazarus was sick, he stayed where he was two more days" (John 11:5–6, italics added).

At this, Brandi again began weeping. "Why did He wait, Ele? Why? Didn't He know how much Mary needed Him . . . how they *all* needed Him . . . how much *I* need Him?"

"Yes, Brandi, He knew . . . and He knows. As hard as it is to understand and accept, Jesus *chose* to wait. He purposed to wait," I explained.

When Brandi calmed down again, she picked up reading in John 11:

On his arrival [at the home of Mary, Martha, and Lazarus], Jesus found that Lazarus had already been in the tomb for four days. Bethany was less than two miles from Jerusalem, and many Jews had come to Martha and Mary to comfort them in the loss of their brother. When Martha heard that Jesus was coming, she went out to meet him, *but Mary stayed at home.* (John 11:17–20, italics added)

"Brandi, why do you think Mary stayed home?" I gently inquired. After another moment of silence, she replied, "Because the one she most counted on was not there when she desperately needed Him. She felt lonely, tricked, and empty, and she probably didn't want to be further disappointed."

"I think that is exactly how Mary was feeling at that time," I responded. "She must have felt betrayed and most assuredly devalued by Jesus. Why, I'm sure she thought that since they were so loved by Jesus, He would rush to their side to prevent any pain from invading their lives."

"Uh-huh," came over the phone line. I could sense Brandi's head slowly nodding in affirmation.

"When did Mary go to Jesus?" I asked. Brandi read on in the passage until she came to verse 28. "'The Teacher is here,' [Martha] said, 'and is asking for you.' When Mary heard this, she got up quickly and went to him."

"The passage says that she responded to Him asking for her," Brandi concluded.

"Yes, it does," I agreed. "What do you think was going on inside Mary at that time?" I wondered.

After a pause Brandi ventured, "She was hurt, very hurt by the absence of Jesus at the time of her extreme need. She probably didn't want to go to Him too quickly, she didn't want to depend on Him too deeply after what He didn't do for her . . . for them . . . after He let them down."

"Would you please read verse 32 out loud for us, Brandi?" She blew her nose, cleared her throat, and read, "When Mary reached the place where Jesus was and saw him, she fell at his feet and said, 'Lord, if you had been here, my brother would not have died.'"

"How does this relate to what you are currently going through?" I inquired.

"I guess that I need to go to Him, fall at His feet, and talk to Him about how I'm feeling," she whispered.

"Are you willing to do just that?" I invited.

"Yes, I am," was her soft response.

And that's exactly what Brandi did. She poured out her heart to Jesus, telling Him exactly how she felt: set up, betrayed, devalued, left alone, hurt, and exposed. Her heart broke before Jesus, and all her sadness, anger, embarrassment, bewilderment, agony, and pain went from her heart to His heart.

It took some time for Brandi to "empty out." My role was to pray silently for her, to stand with her in her deep time of multidimensional need. No words from me were needed or wanted. I was on holy ground, witnessing the purest form of interchange between a follower of Jesus and Jesus Himself. Nothing else was necessary.

When Brandi's intimate time with Jesus was over, I gently asked her to read on. She read, in John 11:33–35, these incredible words: "[Jesus] was deeply moved in spirit and troubled. 'Where have you laid [Lazarus]?' he asked. 'Come and see, Lord,' they replied. Jesus wept."

"Brandi, what is Jesus' response to Mary, to her agony, to her weeping?"

After a pause I barely heard her answer, "He was deeply moved in spirit and troubled."

"Yes," I agreed, "He was. Mary's pain affected Jesus. He felt the depth of her disappointment in Him. He realized how very lonely and devalued she felt by His absence. He was deeply moved in spirit, and He was troubled as well. And then what did Jesus do, Brandi?"

"It says that 'Jesus wept,'" she replied.

"Brandi, why was Jesus weeping?"

At this Brandi again paused. I could almost feel her thinking through the question. "I've heard it said that He was weeping for Lazarus, but that just doesn't make any sense to me. He *knew* Lazarus was going to die. He purposefully waited until he did die! Why weep for Lazarus?" Then I heard a catch in her voice, an "aha" moment. The Spirit was being who the Spirit is, her Teacher and Counselor. "Why, He was weeping *with Mary*! He was weeping *for Mary*! He was identifying with the pain and grief *that He had imposed on Mary*! He loved her. He knew the depth of her agony, and He was weeping with Mary." At this revelation both Brandi and I began weeping as well. Jesus knew! Jesus cared! Jesus was calling Brandi to come to Him. Jesus "saw her weeping" and was "deeply moved in spirit and troubled" as a result.

The living water of truth flowed freely over Brandi's troubled soul. The grace of Jesus Himself was cleansing Brandi's mind, will, and emotions. Truth had been infused into her reality and her reality was adjusting to the purity of that holy invasion.

That phone call was a pivotal conversation in the marriage of Brandi and Gene. Gene still struggles with his addition to pornography. The consequences of his sin continue to infect their relationship. But Brandi knows that Jesus cares, that Jesus says, "This sickness will not end in death. No, it is for God's glory so that God's Son may be glorified through it" (John 11:4).

Brandi has had to rethink how she sees Jesus. Her focus is now on Him and not on her husband. Gene has chosen to take a quiet route with his situation. Brandi has chosen to continue her walk in truth with Jesus. She continues to identify with Mary of Bethany, who "took about a pint of pure nard, an expensive perfume; she poured it on Jesus' feet and wiped his feet with her hair. And the house was filled with the fragrance of the perfume" (John 12:3). That's exactly what Brandi is choosing to do as well—to pour out the most expensive part of her life on Jesus' feet, so that her house is filled with the fragrance of the perfume. Her life is well invested in Him.

14

Variations of the same theme

Spiritual mentoring is a fun, varied, and unexpected journey at times. Just as in any journey, there are twists and turns that one could never anticipate at the offset. At the beginning of any journey, there are assumptions and expectations that are likely. However, in the life of a spiritual mentor, there are encounters and relationships that could never be foreseen. Jesus will say, "What you are doing is great! Now, permit Me to interject this other person into your life. Are you willing?"

There's the rub: being willing. Some of the women who will want you to mentor them will be a surprise to you. Some will be welcome. Some may not be as welcome. However, if the spiritual mentor is in tune with the Source, those "bumps in the road" of the traveler will be seen as "divine encounters" of the best kind! Allow me to illustrate one such encounter.

Kristina and I were greeters together at our church. We enjoyed standing at the open door of the building where the church meets. We would offer handshakes to the guys and give warm hugs to the women as they entered. During the lulls of the ebb and flow of people coming, Kristina and I would chat about life, about this incident and that option.

It was always fun to be a greeter with Kristina.

I liked Kristina from the beginning. She has a midforties figure that shows the wear and tear of multiple children passing through it. She wears glasses for seeing, not as a fashion statement. Her dark brown hair is thick and wavy, and she keeps it under control with a no-nonsense cut. She is the mother of four. Two are grown, married, and out of the house. The other two are very active teenagers who keep their mother busy with a host of errands and activities. Kristina is a great multitasker who loves Jesus. She is also a friend.

Kristina emails. She loves to send text messages as well. In that regard she's a bit "out there" for other moms in her circle. She is always forwarding some interesting bit of news or information. So when I saw her name pop up on my email, I was all ready to receive some helpful tidbit or to laugh at some crazy forwarded message.

This email was different. It was a request for me to consider mentoring her. My first response was, "Why?" It seemed to me that we were more friends than mentor and mentee, and I, frankly, didn't want to upset that pleasant balance. I dutifully wrote her and shared with her that, like anyone else who wanted to be mentored, I would ask her to pray about it for one week. I would do the same. After that we would compare notes to see if we were on the same page or not. I assumed the "or not" would be our mutual conclusion.

However, as prayer overtook my personal slant on the situation, I could sense the Spirit saying, "Ele, walk with Kristina on her journey. Share some of Kristina's joy and some of her pain on a deeper level. I would like you to 'be' in her life." So, at the end of our week of prayer, we both were able to confirm that indeed, yes, the Spirit was calling both of us to be cotravelers together.

Our first meeting was at a Starbucks. We got in line and she started talking at once. Kristina is a talker; there is no doubt about that. As the line inched forward, she was wondering out loud about all the specials that were handwritten on Starbucks' chalkboard. However, she was talking about the colors and handwriting flairs, not the actual beverage choices! Yes, that's Kristina!

We were nearing the front of the line. The moment I like best at Starbucks was coming: the moment when the person behind the counter makes eye contact with *you*, when he or she welcomes *you* to Starbucks, and when "May I take *your* order?" is addressed to *you*! The moment came for us. To no one's surprise, Al, the guy behind the counter, looked at me and said, "Hi, Ele. Do you want your regular soy, no water, no foam chai . . . grande?"

Did I want my usual? Does the world turn on its axis during a twenty-four hour period? "Yeah, Al, that would be great!" I replied, all filled up with knowing that I was known and that my beverage would be served exactly like I loved it. Kristina was equally well known and highly thought of at this particular Starbucks as well. After picking up our beverages, we went outside and found a quiet table.

Kristina seemed excited. Evidently she had heard from other women I mentor, and she was ready to begin her own adventure with Jesus. We began talking. Up until then, Kristina and I had been accustomed to chatting—to talking about TV shows and commenting on daily events. But Kristina was ready to talk. There were some things on her heart that she needed and wanted to share. So she began to share on that level. And I began to listen.

An interesting phenomenon occurs when a person wants to be mentored. There's a door within them that opens, an expectation that arises, a hope that allows itself to breathe, sighing, "Ah, at last. Someone is going to care for me. Someone will be there for me. Someone will be helping to carry my burden. I welcome this person into my life on that level." What also lifts its delicate head with big saucer eyes is the deepest part of them whispering, "And may that someone be worthy. May that person not betray me. May I be safe with that person. Please, God, may I be safe."

Kristina and I had just crossed the threshold between friendship and mentorship. I felt the weight of what she was sharing shift a bit from her shoulders to mine. Our times together had begun.

After about an hour of sharing some of her life story, the flow of Kristina's narrative slowed. I sensed that the first round of exhaling was nearing its end. As with other mentees, I've noted that things have got to *get out* before the mentees are ready to receive. This is a huge factor in effective spiritual mentoring: allowing "stuff" to get out and be heard before there is a prayer of a chance that that person will be able to receive any input of any substance. Kristina was nearing that point. She had been heard, and she was still accepted. The time had now arrived that we, together, could begin to grow in Jesus.

As with others, I had Kristina turn to the gospel of John. She had been part of God's family for several years, so she knew where to find the book of John. Kristina read—out loud—a portion of that first chapter and then we reviewed it together. She went home from that time together with a lighter load than when she had arrived. She also went home with new insights about Jesus. Her journey was going and growing.

The next few times with Kristina went well. She always came prepared and had much to share about the text as well as about her personal life. I could almost visibly see Kristina growing. And then she seemed to hit a brick wall when we came to John 1:43–49. In this passage of Scripture, we read the following situation:

> The next day Jesus decided to leave for Galilee. Finding Philip, he said to him, "Follow me." . . . Philip found Nathanael and told him, "We have found the one Moses wrote about in the Law, and about whom the prophets also wrote—Jesus of Nazareth, the son of Joseph." "Nazareth! Can anything good come from there?" Nathanael asked. "Come and see," said Philip. When Jesus saw Nathanael approaching, he said of him, "Here is a true Israelite, in whom there is nothing false." "How do you know me?" Nathanael asked. Jesus answered, "I saw you while you were still under the fig tree before Philip called you." Then Nathanael declared, "Rabbi, you are the Son of God; you are the King of Israel."

The thought was introduced that when Philip invited Nathanael to "come and see," Nathanael's reply was anything but open. "Can anything good come out of Nazareth?" Nathanael revealed a snobbish attitude, an "I don't think so" mind-set. That part was okay with Kristina. She had not only heard that way of thinking from others, she, at times, had shared that point of view herself.

What irked Kristina was the manner in which Jesus dealt with him. Actually, better said, it was the manner in which Jesus *didn't* deal with him. We see this in verse 47: "When Jesus saw Nathanael approaching, he said of him, 'Here is a true Israelite, in whom there is nothing false.'" We see Jesus, who knows everything (which He demonstrated in verse 48), choosing to ignore Nathanael's snobbish attitude and, instead, deciding to compliment him. It blew Kristina's mind that Jesus looked beyond the smart remark to *the intent* of the remark. She couldn't believe that the first thing out of Jesus' mouth was a compliment. Jesus could have chosen to condemn, to correct, or to corner Nathanael by using Nathanael's own sharp words against him. Rather than those options, however, Jesus chose to hear the intent of what Nathanael meant to say instead of what he actually said. The gift of knowing the intent of the heart that Jesus gave to Nathanael marked a pivotal point in Nathanael's life. He was then free to quickly declare, "Rabbi, you are the Son of God, you are the King of Israel" (John 1:49). Jesus is exactly who He claims to be!

Kristina and I discussed how to bring others to Jesus, the importance of hearing the intent of the heart rather than the wording in the moment, and of leading with grace and having truth follow (as seen in John 1:13). Another aspect of this passage we discussed was how there are certain things that we are responsible for in the life of another, and, conversely, there are things that we are not responsible for as well. We saw Philip inviting Nathanael to "come and see" (John 1:46). We did not see Philip trying to convince Nathanael or to debate with him. We didn't see Philip correcting Nathanael or being embarrassed by Nathanael's quick statement. Philip simply invited Nathanael to "come and see," period.

Kristina's face scrunched up as she listened. She was moving back and forth in her seat, twirling the green straw in the lid of her Starbucks cup. Kristina was clearly agitated.

"Okay, let's talk about this," she stated.

"All right, let's," I agreed.

"Well," Kristina wondered, "how does this apply to my own kids— my grown kids—the two who are out of the house and on their own?"

Kristina had asked me a great question. Part of the principle we see here is that Philip didn't try to convince, correct, or debate Nathanael. He simply handed Nathanael an invitation to "come and see."

"What are you thinking, Kristina? Are there things in another's life that you are carrying that you shouldn't be carrying?" I asked.

Kristina thought for a moment before answering. "I'm not sure. I sure do want my grown kids to 'come and see' Jesus for themselves, especially my daughter. Her oldest sibling is doing fine with Jesus, but Karley is having trouble. A lot of her trouble is her own making. She grew up in the church and is now rethinking much of what she was taught. She's like Nathanael in that way, with that 'can anything good come from there' type of outlook."

"How can you best partner with who the Holy Spirit is being in her life?" I queried.

"I *knew* you were going to ask me that!" Kristina exclaimed, laughing. "You know, I'm not really sure. I know that I talk to her *a lot* about her 'relationship with Jesus.' She assures me that they're 'tight' and that I shouldn't stress over it so much. I guess that I need to focus more on hearing the intent of my daughter's heart and lavishing more grace on her rather than riding her so hard."

"Seems like a good idea to me," I responded. "I bet that Karley would also like that! Would you like to begin putting that principle into practice this week?" Kristina slowly nodded her head in agreement. "Okay then, let's talk about how that principle can be fleshed out between Karley and you."

Kristina took it to heart and began to back off from nagging her daughter so much about her church attendance. Instead, Kristina started to throw out open-ended thoughts and ideas about Jesus in the conversations that she had with Karley. Kristina was determined to say nothing about Karley's lack of attending church and to focus on the

"Jesus" in Karley. And Karley immediately noticed the difference in her mom.

The two of them began to have open discussions about spiritual matters. It was a pleasant surprise to Kristina to realize that Karley was interested, very interested actually, in growing spiritually. Karley just wasn't crazy about what the established church had evolved into. She was searching for relationship, not the polished performances and slick speeches that were presented each week. She wanted truth in her reality, not a "quick fix" for the week. And Jesus was in full agreement with that!

Several months went by when, upon opening my email account, I found an email from Karley. She was very excited about the change in her mom and how now they could talk about spiritual things without her mom becoming all "mom-ish." Karley went on to say, "I am seeing such a transformation in my own mom that I'm wondering if you would be able to meet with me as well. I really want to grow in my faith and have no idea how to."

I was so surprised that I laughed out loud. "Jesus, are You really wanting me to walk alongside of a mother and a daughter at the same time?" Well, after Karley and I prayed about it for a week, we found ourselves at Starbucks and opening up the living Word of God as Karley began the journey of going from who she was to who she wanted to be in Jesus! Isn't that amazing? It was a variation on the same theme of being a spiritual mentor.

You might think this is an isolated case. Let me assure you that it isn't. The Lord has brought other mother/daughter situations into my life. And, as with each and every relationship in mentoring, *confidentiality* has the highest priority. I state this to all the women I mentor: I will pray for them daily, and I will not talk about them to anyone, including my husband. That is why all of the women mentioned in this book are composites. They are not real women, but they represent the experiences, struggles, and joys of real women.

Your mentees *must* have the assurance and safety that what they share with you will remain confidential, or authentic mentoring will not happen. This is particularly true when you are mentoring more than one woman. Whether they are relatives, good friends, or total strangers, they *must* be assured that whatever they share with you stays with you and you alone.

I'd like to illustrate to you another "variation of the same theme" as far as mentoring goes. The Lord has also brought some women of other cultures and nationalities across my path. When we as spiritual mentors are honored with walking alongside of women from other countries or cultural backgrounds, we need to be particularly sensitive to share *principles* from the Word of God rather than *examples* of how to apply scriptural principles. For some of us it is easy to confuse the two: principles and applications of those principles.

One thing that I just love about the Word of God is that it is "living and active," as stated in Hebrews 4:12. The principles of the Word of God can be absorbed into any fiber of every culture. The colors of the threads and the pattern that emerges from the weave are as varied as the breath of the Holy Spirit moving over Christ-followers in those cultures. The principles of the Word of God are the same no matter where you live. However, living out those principles may look quite different in other cultures than it does in our own. The wise spiritual mentor knows this and doesn't try to impose her own culture upon her mentee. What an exciting adventure for the two of you if the Lord allows you the honor of coming alongside a sister from another cultural point of view!

Enjoy each and every "variation on the same theme" in your adventure as a spiritual mentor. Remember to come alongside of these women, enhancing who the Holy Spirit is being in their lives, partnering with the Holy Spirit by infusing truth into their realities in an appropriate and timely manner. Pray daily for those you mentor, taking them and their life situations to the throne of grace and leaving them there. Keep what they share with you close to your heart. It is *their* story to share, not yours. As you do so, the Holy Spirit will entrust to you exactly whom He desires. That is an extreme joy and privilege. What an honor it is to be the junior partner in all varieties of mentoring relationships!

15

Another
road taken

We had been meeting for nearly six months when Brenda dropped the bomb. Brenda is a thirtysomething single woman living at home with her parents. She has a good job, a smooth-running sports car, money in the bank, and a growing passion for Jesus. She is one of the thousands of Generation Xers who grew up going to church and most of its activities, was sent to a Christian school, and, upon graduating, decided quite openly not to continue going to church. Now, at age thirtysomething, Brenda is still posing the same questions she did back then. "Why should I go to church?" she asked me one day. "None of my friends go. I know the stories, and frankly, it just doesn't do anything for me anymore." She's quick to add that she still believes in Jesus and wants to grow in Him. "Just leave the church thing out of the equation" is her request.

So we did. Brenda and I were sipping our caramel macchiatos together at Starbucks. We were looking at the account of the woman caught in the act of adultery in John 8:1–11. Brenda was reading the account out loud, and she got to verses 10 and 11 where it says, "Jesus straightened up and asked her, 'Woman, where are they? Has no one condemned you?' 'No one, sir,' she said. 'Then neither do I condemn you,' Jesus declared. 'Go now and leave your life of sin.'"

Brenda paused in her reading. She looked up, but not at me. I sensed that she was revisiting a time and place in her own past. After a few moments she quietly said, "I can relate to that woman."

Brenda was a thinker. She weighed options. She was not a quick decision maker. She mulled and pondered. That's what I loved most about Brenda—her thinking process. Most of her life her thinking process had been short-circuited. Since she didn't verbalize her thoughts, most people wrote her off as a too-quiet, very shy gal without much to contribute. The exact opposite was true. Those who invested time in her, sharing the pauses and not pushing for premature conclusions, were rewarded with depth, insight, and conviction. She needed a spiritual mentor in her life, and I was the one she had requested. What an honor!

We continued sitting there. Brenda was thinking about that woman who, so long ago, had been humiliated, shamed, and exposed in the most intimate of ways . . . and Brenda has just confessed that she could relate to her.

What should I do? After sending up a quick prayer to our Teacher, I asked her, "Do you want to talk about it?" Yes, she did.

Brenda began telling me that after high school she met a guy named Jim. He was an "all right guy"; she liked him, more than other guys. When he asked her to move in with him, she had said, "Okay." Life with Jim was predictable. Brenda liked that. It made her feel safe. So she kept on feeling safe with Jim for five years. Then one day Jim announced that he was bored with her and that she needed to move on. It was a wake-up call to Brenda, but one that she had known was coming. So she moved out of Jim's place and back in with her mom and dad. She was doing okay there, for although her parents were both believers in Jesus, they were dealing with their own disappointments. Often Brenda and her mom would go outside on the patio, share a smoke, and talk about life. That worked for both of them, or so it seemed. Then Joe entered her life.

Joe was everything that Jim was not. Joe was an engaging conversationalist, a good listener, he loved people, and he actually liked Brenda's parents! The four of them soon became dating couples. Brenda enjoyed hanging out together like that.

Since Brenda and I had started meeting, she had shared with me about her sex life. She was obviously no longer a virgin. Jim was not the first she had been with, just the longest. And now Joe was in her life. Hence the comment, "I can relate to that woman." "How can you relate to her?" I inquired.

"Well," Brenda said, "it says that she was caught in adultery. So she probably really loved the guy. I'm not sure she was a prostitute like I've heard so often. It might be that she was married to some jerk and she was having an affair with someone she really cared about!"

"Yes," I agreed. "It could have been that way. How does that make you feel?" I queried.

Brenda put her head down a bit, sipped more of her macchiato, and replied, "Sad. I feel sad for her. Here she thought she had found someone who loved her and it was a setup all along."

Spirit, I prayed, *where are we going with this*? To the woman sitting across from me, I said, "Brenda, have *you* ever felt set up?"

There was a long pause . . . an uncomfortable pause . . . a *Spirit, help her*! kind of pause. Then she started talking.

"You know, when I was a kid I never thought my life would turn out the way that it has so far. I thought that I would grow up, meet the man of my dreams, and get married . . . after lots of fooling around, partying every weekend, and buying a bunch of stuff for myself!" Brenda laughed at the memory of the dream. Her laugh softened into a smile, the upper right corner of her mouth slightly turning up. "This is kind of weird to say, but I still have part of my little girl dream in my head."

"You do?" I responded, smiling. "What part is it?"

"Well, now don't laugh, but I have this dream that my guy will get down on one knee and have a huge ring—the *right* huge ring—and that he will make the most imaginative and wonderful proposal known to womankind. My wedding gown will be a one-of-a-kind, incredibly super dress, and I will be a knockout in it. We'll have the most expensive wedding ever with everything we want, and we'll go on an out-of-this-world honeymoon. Then we'll come home together to a neat house that we'll pick out together, furnish together, and live in together . . . forever!" Brenda was out of breath when she finished relating her dream.

"I like it, I really do!" I shared, and we laughed together. "Now tell me this, Brenda," I said, "which part of the dream is still alive?"

At this, shadows began to cloud her once-bright face. "Oh, it's all just a little girl's fantasy," was her barely audible reply. "What makes it just a little girl's fantasy?" I asked. Brenda didn't answer right away. She was thinking. That was good. An honest answer would be forthcoming. "I've already told you that I'm not a virgin," she began. "That ideal went out the door in 1996, the year of 'Tony the Tiger.' That's what we girls called him. I was one of his trophy girls. What a schmuck he was! But I really don't count him. There were others, and then, of course, Jim. What a royal jerk!" She paused, remembering some past wrongs done to her by Jim. "But now Joe is in my life," Brenda perked up, "and things are so great between us."

"What makes it great between the two of you?" I wondered.

"Joe is very into family. I love that! He's funny, very good-looking, my parents like him, *I* like him!" Brenda laughed at that. "He's one of the 'good guys.' He treats me well. Oh, and he's starting to go to church with me!" she announced.

"Wow! That is something! I didn't realize that *you* were attending church, either. How long has this been?" I questioned.

"Oh, not that long. But we do go together now, and sometimes we even talk about what was shared."

"From where I'm sitting, things sound good, Brenda," I offered.

"Yeah, they are. But there's still that dream that I would like to hold on to."

"And what's that?" I asked.

"It's the part where we wait until we're married and then come together as husband and wife for the first time." There. She had said it. *That* was what her dream was.

"That's a very incredibly wonderful dream you have there, Brenda,"

I replied. "What would keep you from having it all?"

Brenda bit her lower lip, a nervous habit that she had. "Joe," she almost whispered. "Joe wants me to move in with him . . . now."

My heart sank. It sank for Brenda, for the little girl inside of her that wanted the dream—God's dream—for her. And it was being jeopardized by the one Brenda loved, Joe.

"Have the two of you talked about this?" I wondered.

"Oh my, yes, have we. I tell him that we should wait. My plan is that if we pool our money, we could get married within the year."

"And how does he feel about that?" I asked

"Well," volunteered Brenda, "he's not crazy about waiting. He thinks it's outdated, stupid, and unreasonable, to use his words."

"How do *you* feel about it, Brenda?" I gently asked.

Without hesitating she said, "I'd like to wait."

The conversation went back to the woman caught in adultery. Brenda was especially intrigued as to what Jesus said to the woman when all the guys had gone. Jesus said, "'Woman, where are they? Has no one condemned you?' 'No one, sir,' she said. 'Then neither do I condemn you,' Jesus declared. 'Go now and leave your life of sin'" (John 8:10–11). I asked Brenda, "Would you consider leaving your life of sin?"

I would like to be able to say that Brenda, after thinking about it, did wait to have sexual relations with Joe until they were married. However, that isn't what happened. A few meetings later Brenda announced that she had moved in with Joe. They are still attending church services together. They are still spending time with her folks. But Brenda let go of her dream. She silently tucked away the little girl within her and, after considering, chose not to leave her life of sin. Another road was taken.

So, spiritual mentor, what is our position when one of our mentees decides to take another road? Do we dump them? Do we ignore the issue? Do we tell someone else what's going on? I would propose that we keep on keeping on with them . . . *just the way the Holy Spirit does with us!* We can do no less than that. We stick with them. We pray for them daily, we maintain meeting with them, we keep taking them to Jesus, and we consistently come alongside of them and partner with who the

Spirit is being in their lives. We don't give up. We don't nag. We don't scold. We hold nothing over their heads—no guilt, no shame. We purpose to continue to infuse truth into their reality with openness, friendship, kindness, and acceptance. We persist in joining the Spirit in gently saying, "Would you consider leaving your life of sin now?" After all, the Spirit gently offers the same to *us* every day.

16

Mandy

I first noticed Mandy's daughter before I noticed Mandy. Missy is a laid-back, full-faced two-year-old who is one of those kids every preschool teacher wants to have in her classroom. Missy is gentle, slow-moving, and long-suffering as far as being shoved around is concerned. When one of the boys whizzes by her and grabs a small toy car out of her hand, Missy stands there as if evaluating the situation, and she decides that the better choice would be to go get another toy rather than to fuss about it. Missy is a nice little girl.

Mandy is a grown-up Missy. Mandy is a rather large woman, her fine, straight true-blonde hair pulled back in a tight ponytail. Her clothes hang loosely over her large frame. Mandy is one of those women who would probably be chosen last if she were at a softball game instead of a baby shower. She has a full face, an honest face, a face that one could take advantage of if one wanted to. I didn't want to. I wanted to be Mandy's friend.

As I looked around the room at the baby shower, I saw groups of young women naturally forming conversational circles. There seems to be an invisible magnet that pulls some women together and, conversely, keeps others from entering the circle. Mandy wasn't in one of those circles, and she seemed to be overly preoccupied with her beverage and cake. I realized that she was employing the "beverage and cake move." This move is one that many women use at social gatherings when the moment is awkward. We use the "beverage and cake move" when we want to enter into an ongoing conversation, such as, "Oh, excuse me, but do you know if it's all right to help ourselves to the beverage and cake?" We also use the move when we are feeling uncomfortable, on the verge of being left standing alone by ourselves, when everyone else is busily chatting in a group. Helping ourselves to the beverage and cake is a legitimate move at any social function for women. Other women know the move and graciously allow the person to enter into the magnetic circle or silently avert their eyes as another suffers alone with her cake and beverage in hand. As I said, the "beverage and cake move" was being employed by Mandy. She was obviously feeling a bit left out of the huddle, and with good reason; she *was* being left out.

"Aren't you Missy's mom?" I quietly asked Mandy. "Uh, why, yes, I am," replied Mandy with that knowing "thank-you" look in her eyes. She had been saved from the discomfort of "the after." "The after" happens when the "beverage and cake move" has been completed and the realization dawns that something has to be resolved or the person will be left in social limbo. It's a horrible place to be, especially at a baby shower. "How do you know Missy?" she questioned. Well, I really didn't know Missy at all. I had seen Missy in the nursery on the few occasions when I had deposited my two-year-old grandson at the door. I had caught Missy's name on the back of her dress as she was fending off some rather ambitious little boys in the classroom. That was my extent of knowing Missy. But it was enough to get a conversation going with Mandy.

I found that Mandy was a delightful person; she was quick-witted, intelligent, a lover of science, and the owner of two large cats and an even bigger dog. Mandy, Missy, the cats and dog, along with her husband of nearly three years, Tad, lived together in a duplex on the other side of the city. She was a diamond in the rough.

We enjoyed each other's company at the baby shower. Mandy's gift was homemade, I noted. It was a generic notebook that Mandy had covered by decoupaging a book-sized piece of wallpaper onto the front and back covers and applying some braiding as decoration. She had also decorated a pen by attaching a silk flower to it with green florist's tape. The combination made a lovely journal and pen for the young mother-to-be. The gift was graciously received.

A few days after the shower, my phone rang. Mandy wanted to know if I would be willing to meet with her as a spiritual mentor. I had promised myself that I would not add any more mentees to my life at that point. Each woman is so unique and deserves time and energy from her mentor, and I didn't think I could take on another one. But I felt like I needed to seek the Spirit's guidance, so we decided that both of us would dedicate time to pray for one week to see if it was of the Lord or not. I could hear Mandy's hope over the phone. She needed the right mentor, but I wasn't convinced that I was the one for her.

A week went by and it was time to talk to Mandy again. I'm so thankful for the confirmation of prayer to do or not to do something because it was with a full heart that I was able to accept her invitation to be a part of her life. Spiritual mentoring had begun.

Our first meeting was at Mandy's home. The duplex was in a crowded part of the city. Traffic noise entered through the open front window. The small living room boasted an old sofa, two mismatched overstuffed chairs, a table, and two lamps. I was invited to sit on the sofa. The large dog that was part of Mandy's entourage seemed eager to be part of the mentoring process. He jumped up next to me and plopped down as I sat on the sagging sofa. "He probably smells my dog, Winston," I nervously explained as Teddy sniffed me from head to toe. "What a friendly dog you have, Mandy," I observed uneasily. "Get down from there, Teddy!" ordered Mandy. Either Teddy was a deaf dog or slow to follow commands, for soon he was curled up, half of him beside me and the other half on top of me, snoring contentedly as we began our time together. I was one of the family.

"Tell me about yourself," I said, beginning the conversation.

"Well, there's really not a whole lot to tell," Mandy said thoughtfully. "Let's see. I was raised in a family of six. I have three brothers, one older and two younger. I'm the only girl in the family, the rose among all those thorns!" She nervously laughed. "My brothers all still live at home with my mom and dad. I work part-time at the observatory right up the street from the church. That's how I began attending the church; I drove by it every day, and after a while I started attending. Tad and I have been married nearly three years. And in case you're wondering, Missy was almost a honeymoon baby. Not quite but almost." She was right. I had wondered.

The conversation seemed a bit stilted, but it was the first time other than the baby shower that Mandy and I had conversed. Her sharing was brief and sketchy. I passed it off as nerves since she didn't know me very well. We began our study in John, and it went fine. She understood. Her scientific mind played and replayed John 1:3, "Through him all things were made; without him nothing was made that has been made."

I was seeing a bit more into who Mandy was. She was a deep thinker. A still, untapped pool lay beneath her big eyes, beneath the soft natural-blonde hair that was pulled tightly up into a ponytail. Time with Mandy was going to be interesting.

As we began to meet on a somewhat regular basis, I began to note some of Mandy's social habits. She usually sat with her back to the majority of the other customers if we met in a restaurant. Her posture was "soft" in that she rounded her shoulders, thus drawing into herself. At times I had to look down and then up over the rim of my reading glasses in order to make eye contact with Mandy. She was shy and soft-spoken when we were in public, but when we met at her home she came alive, greeting me with a full-faced smile that would light her up from the top of her head to the bottom of her toes. Mandy was always prepared for our time together. She wrote pages and pages of thoughts and answers to the questions that we found in the gospel of John. Her responses were full of thought, insight, and even humor at times. Mandy was truly hungry and thirsty after right living. She was blossoming before my very eyes.

"It" happened when we were studying John 2:12–16. We were reading the account where Jesus went up to the temple and there found "men selling cattle, sheep and doves, and others sitting at tables exchanging money. So he made a whip out of cords, and drove all from the temple area. . . . to those who sold doves he said, 'Get these out of here! How dare you turn my Father's house into a market!'" (John 2:14–16). The words of Jesus were appropriately harsh. The purpose for His "Father's house" was not being honored. It was to be a "house of prayer" but it had been turned into a "den of robbers" (Luke 19:46).

I asked Mandy, "What is the temple of God now? Is it a building? What does the Word of God say the temple of God is now?" She tipped her head to the left, rolling her eyes up as she searched her memory for the correct answer. In order to help the process, I asked her to look up 1 Corinthians 6:19. She found the passage and began to read out loud. "Do you not know that *your body* is a temple of the Holy Spirit, who is in you, whom you have received from God?" (italics added). There was a long pause as Mandy seemed to leave the present, fixing her eyes on a scene in her memory. She stared at it, not moving. The long pause was joined by one single tear that began coursing its way down her right cheek. The pause continued as Mandy focused on the memory.

I was unsure what to do. I knew something incredibly painful was occurring inside of her. "Mandy, what is it?" I found myself whispering to her. I reached over, putting my hand on top of hers. She quickly pulled her hand back as if I had slapped her. "Mandy, what is it?" I repeated. She slowly pulled her eyes from the scene running through her mind and focused them on her hand. "I can't be a follower of Jesus anymore," she said in a flat, voiceless tone.

Where did that come from, Jesus? I prayed. *Help me partner with who You are in her life, right now, Jesus. We both need Your help, Holy Spirit!*

Time passed and we sat as the gravity of the moment began to weigh us down. "Mandy, is there something you would like to share with me?" I gently invited. She continued to sit across from me but I knew she was a long way off, in another time of her life. Then she slowly began to share her story.

"It began one night when I was at a sleepover at my aunt and uncle's home," Mandy began. "My brothers and I had stayed over plenty of other times. This night started out like any of those other visits. We kids played hide-and-seek in the backyard while the adults sat inside, drinking a few beers and playing cards. We all were called in after it got too dark to see to play. Then it was time to go to bed. My brothers and my boy cousins slept sprawled all over my one cousin's bedroom. They would have pillow fights and let out war whoops until my aunt told them to quiet down. I slept in the living room on the sofa, since I was the only girl.

"That night my uncle tiptoed over to the sofa and sort of messed with my hair. It woke me up. I gave him a sleepy smile and he smiled back as I rolled over to go back to sleep. I thought he was up to get a drink of water or go to the bathroom, since it was the middle of the night. But then he touched my shoulder and kept that smile on his face, and then he . . ." Mandy's voice broke and her eyes swiftly riveted back from the memory of that first violation, that painful betrayal, to the present moment with me.

"Ele, he raped me. My uncle raped me. And I was only a little girl! Why would he do that?" And then the tears came. Shame, disappointment, disgust, anger, and hate poured out of her shattered heart. "That was the first time, but not the only time he did that to me. I guess I could have stopped him. I wanted to. I hate him! I hate all of them: my uncle, the boys, my aunt, my parents . . . they all knew and yet no one stopped it. Ele," she took at deep breath and then blurted out, "I'm the awful family secret!" Mandy sat there numbed, frozen, and hardened by her own words.

God, help me! my heart cried out. *Help me help Mandy. Touch her, help her through Your Word*! But it was the Word that was causing Mandy such deep anguish of heart and soul. "Ele, if my body is a temple of the Holy Spirit and any misuse of that temple makes Jesus rightly angry, I can't be a follower of Jesus anymore!" And the tears returned, her eyes reddening in the flow.

This was a huge moment in Mandy's life. This was pivotal. Truth *had* to be infused—correctly—into her reality. The Holy Spirit had chosen this moment to begin to set Mandy free from her past. "Mandy,"

I began gently, "thank you for entrusting your past to me. You have carried this overwhelming burden by yourself far too long. Let's return to the Word of God and see exactly what it is saying and what it is not saying, okay?" Mandy nodded ever so slightly. What a brave moment this was in her life! We returned to the passage in John 2:13–16 that had opened the door to this particular situation. "Mandy, please read the text over again, out loud," I requested.

Mandy read the verses again. "Now let's take a look at what was going on, shall we?" I suggested. She again nodded ever so slightly. "Here we see several things. First, Jesus is going to the temple, probably to pray, for that was the temple's intended use, as we saw in Luke 19:46. But instead of finding a place suitable for prayer, He entered into a situation that was entirely inappropriate for the temple. *Intruders* were there, trespassers who were there *taking advantage* of the place of worship and prayer. So we see Jesus doing the most appropriate thing He could do: He made a whip and 'drove all from the temple area, both sheep and cattle,' the account tells us (John 2:15). *He didn't condemn the temple; He drove out those who were misusing the temple.* There's a huge difference between the two. Jesus was actually advocating for the temple; He was stepping in and taking authority over what went on in the temple. Remember, He ordered, 'Get these out of here! How dare you turn my Father's house into a market!' (John 2:16). Jesus knew what should take place in the temple. He understood the importance of the temple. He also knew that others could take advantage of the temple. He saw the situation, stepped in, and *cleansed* the temple.

"Mandy, that's exactly what He is offering *you*! You are correct in saying that your body is now a temple of the Holy Spirit. You are incorrect in assuming that the Holy Spirit wants nothing to do with you. It's actually just the opposite. He wants *everything* to do with you, so much so that He desires to reside within you!

"Jesus sees that young girl trapped in an unholy situation. Mandy, He grieves with you over the abuse and misuse of you ... your body ... His temple. He has 'found men selling cattle, sheep and doves, and others sitting at tables exchanging money' inside of you (John 2:14). He sees the filth, the crimes, the intrusion, and the trespassing that has happened in your life. He is now—this very moment—willing to make a 'whip out of cords' and drive 'all from the temple area,' scattering the coins and overturning the tables these violators have left behind. He desires to say to them, 'Get out of here! How dare you!' This is what Jesus is offering you, Mandy. Do you hear any reprimand in His voice? Do you see any disgust for you—His temple—in His actions? Absolutely not! In fact, the disgust, the anger, and the wrath is all focused on the intruders, the violators, *not* on what was being violated!"

I paused and looked at Mandy. This was new to her. The Enemy of her soul had kept her in a prison of lies for over twenty years. The "door" to her soul, the opening to the "temple," had been carefully guarded, surrounded with the thick armor of self-disgust, denial, and suppression. But truth is overwhelming, light is revealing, and a new beginning is irresistible. Mandy was seeing her past from a fresh perspective. She began to believe that maybe Jesus does care. Could it be that the Holy Spirit could counsel her, be her Teacher and constant companion? Mandy was given truth. It has been infused within the deepest, darkest corners of her reality. And there is hope. In fact, Mandy is, week-by-week, finding strength, perspective, grace, and freedom under the guidance of the Holy Spirit through the Word of God. Something that once defined her is now being carefully reduced to an index card in the reference box of memories. She will always carry with her the scars of what was done to her, but she is no longer defined by those actions. She is a temple of the Holy Spirit, cleansed by Him. She is a temple in which He delights to reside.

17

There's Mentoring
. . . and then there's mentoring

entoring, mentor, mentee . . . these words are most likely relatively new to your vocabulary. "Do you have a mentor?" "Are you mentoring?" "Who is your mentor?" These questions are bandied about, heard in the halls of our church buildings, read in the newsletters we hand out, and visualized on the PowerPoint presentations that entertain us as we wait in our seats for the worship service to begin.

Mentoring . . . I'm amazed at how the concept has become so popularized. It's all over the Internet. It's big in the corporate world. Seminars are taught on how to do it. Authors claim that those who read their books are their mentees. And we can even attend training and become a Certified Spiritual Mentor!

What all this tells me is that there's a whole lot of mentoring going on that merits being defined. By now you are beginning to understand my personal definition of mentoring. But let's take a moment to see what others say about this word and this process.

We understand from a bit of study that the first recorded modern usage of the word *mentor* can be traced to a book entitled *Les Aventures de Télémaque,* by French writer François Fénelon. The lead character's name in the book is Mentor. The book was published in 1699, and it was very popular during the eighteenth century. The modern application of the word *mentor* can be traced back to this publication. Before this writing, we know that in Greek mythology Odysseus's friend Mentor was the chief educator of Odysseus's son. Mentor sprinkled his wisdom throughout the educational process and birthed the concept of mentoring another person: imparting life wisdom and the application of it to another.

So we can see and understand how some define mentoring as an educational process, centered on imparting skills and information to another. A mentor, then, within this definition, is usually an older person with life experience who shares advice and offers support to someone younger or less experienced. As a support to this definition, there are classes in mentoring, internship programs, seminars, workbooks, and other forms of training to prepare the mentor to appropriately train the mentee. This type of mentoring is usually a structured relationship between two people, or between one mentor and a group of people.

Other types of mentoring have also morphed from the original example of an educational process. There are those who see mentoring as having an apprentice: one who closely observes, studies, is given instruction by the mentor, and then is released to put into practice what has been acquired over the instructional time frame. The mentor then becomes a "coach," instructing from the sidelines of life as the mentee begins to live out the game plan sketched out for her by the mentor.

As a result of the mentoring-through-education model, we can see how it was a relatively easy move over to the spiritual part of our lives. We see some people defining spiritual mentoring as a relationship in which the older person, the more experienced mentor, transfers biblical life perspective, principles, spiritual insights, experiences, information, and patterns of living to her mentee in a way that equips and empowers the mentee to apply to her life what the mentor has shared with her. The spiritual mentor's purpose is to empower the mentee to be what God has called her to be and to do.

Others define spiritual mentoring as inviting another to walk alongside of your life, learning from your example, or in other words, being a spiritual companion of another in her life walk.

There are also other words that can be used in place of the word *mentor*, such as *spiritual model, spiritual teacher, spiritual sponsor, spiritual coach, spiritual counselor*, and *discipler*. More than the particular word preference, I firmly believe that the definition of the word needs to be clearly understood before entering into a spiritual mentoring relationship.

Are these definitions important? Probably not. Are the *expectations* behind the philosophies of these definitions noteworthy? Yes, they probably are. My encouragement to you is to invest some alone time before jumping into a mentoring relationship. Ask yourself some of the following questions.

❖ Why do you want to be mentored? Is it being suggested by the women's ministry department of your church? Are other women your age talking it up? Is it an opportunity to get together with others, have child care provided for you, and have some "girl time"? Or are you slowly dying inside wondering if this is all there is to being a follower of Jesus? Are you personally disappointed with what you thought your life was going to be like? Do you hunger for more from Jesus? Why do you want to be mentored?

❖ Whom do you want to mentor you? Does it matter to you? Is it okay with you to be paired up with just anyone? Or is there someone in your life who stands out to you? Is there a woman who is spiritually intriguing to you? Are you attracted to Jesus as a result of knowing a godly woman? Whom do you want to mentor you?

❖ At what life level do you want to be mentored? Do you want a "give me Jesus or I die" level? Do you have an "I'm in for the long haul" mentality? Are you seeing mentoring as a course, a workbook, or a study that lasts for eight weeks? Are you visualizing yourself in a group with other women sharing bits and pieces of life? Are you longing for a safe person with whom to share your life? At what life level do you want to be mentored?

❖ What source do you desire for mentoring? Is a seminar satisfying? Would a study about a book of the Bible be sufficient? Is a workbook suitable? Do you want to wrestle with probing questions about yourself from the living Word of God? Do you long for the Spirit to be your Teacher? Are you ready to enter a classroom of one? What source do you desire for mentoring?

Think through for yourself what outcomes you would like to see in your life as a result of being mentored. As you can see, there are many different definitions for mentoring and for spiritual mentoring. My point is to encourage the prospective mentor and mentee to pause and *clearly define* what you both are anticipating as a result of your time together *before* you enter into a mentoring relationship. Remember, there's mentoring . . . and then there's *mentoring*!

18

And the results are . . . !

*O*ur culture is addicted to results. We even want to know *beforehand* what the results will be, whether it's a movie release, swimming classes, or the presidential election. We're crazy about results. This focus on results has found its way into our local churches as well. In fact, it's rampant. It affects missionary budgets, it influences sermon topics, it determines room usage . . . it's everywhere! We give ourselves away by what we say, don't we? Listen to almost any conversation and you'll hear it. "How many are signed up?" "What was the turnout like?" "How much was given?" "How's registration coming along?" It's all about results.

The same is true for mentoring. People want to know results there too. However, this isn't necessarily a bad thing. Results do have their place. But there are some factors about the *type* of results that need to be addressed. If the results are only determined by numbers, then we're in trouble.

Let's take a look at the "results" of Jesus' ministry. I'm sure you have done this before, but to recap, let's do the math. The Son of God invested three and a half years in ministry. He hung out with a small group of men and women. Twelve of those were His core group, and three in that group were His "inner core" group. At times Jesus spoke to and interacted with the masses of people, but most of His time was invested in the group—the Twelve and the three. And the results were ... that the group disbanded at the beginning of trouble. The Twelve ran off, one of them betraying Jesus in a big way. Out of the "inner core," one denied Him three times in a matter of a few hours. Now, it is true that some of the women were with Him to the end of His death. And a person on the fringe, Nicodemus, got permission to bury His body. That was it— pretty dismal results. Not what you would think of as a winning game plan. There would be no end-of-the-year bonus for those results.

But wait. That's *not* the end of the account. There's more ... *much more!* The women rallied and went to the tomb. Two of the "inner core" followed them. Jesus appeared to the Eleven. And then He appeared to more. He instructed them, reminding them that the things that had happened to Him had to occur. He then left them, but not before telling them that He would send them the Holy Spirit. A few days later the Holy Spirit descended on the believers, and that's when amazing results started occurring. Three thousand became followers of Jesus in one day—three thousand people whose lives were in the process of being transformed, who were beginning their personal journey with the Holy Spirit as their Teacher! And who was the spokesperson? Whom did the Spirit use to speak truth into reality that day? Peter—one of the "inner core"! The one who had denied Jesus just a few weeks earlier. Those were pretty impressive results. In fact, the rest of human history is still being influenced by what occurred that Pentecost morning so long ago!

Results. We want to know results. And for most of us and for the majority of churches, the results are reduced to numbers. How many signed up? How many attended? What is anticipated for next time? We live as if we believe that numbers accurately reflect application of truth to reality.

Don, my husband, and I are part of a local body of believers. Due to our ministries we travel a lot, mostly on weekends. For this reason our attendance at weekend services is sporadic. However, when we are home we do attend. I call it "going to building," not "going to church."

I know, it's a little thing and some may call it childish. Perhaps it is. But I'm attempting to make a point to my inner self. What is the point? The point is that we—the human beings who are followers of Jesus Christ—*are* the church! We don't *go* to church, we *are* the church—the body of Christ. Why do I bring this point up now? Because the results seen in a body are continual, progressive, and slow-growing, not extremely fast.

Don and I love to sharpen one another, as iron sharpens iron. We have often talked about "results" when it comes to church. Here's what typically happens. We, the body, go to services weekly. Someone gets up and talks to us. It usually is very entertaining. It usually is taken from the Word of God. There is almost *always* a "life lesson," something to take home and apply to life during the week. This is good. This is helpful. However, this "life application" is rarely, if ever, followed up on! We attend, we sit, we listen, we receive a challenge, we go home, we live out the week, we return, we sit, we listen . . . I think you get the picture.

Where is the follow-up? Where is the accountability? What are the results? Are the results measured by the attendance? Are the results calculated by the amount of money gathered on any given weekend? Are the results counted by the cars in the parking lot? Are the results accurately reflected in the number of home groups there are at any given moment? How should results be measured?

In dealing with churches and directors of women's ministries, I am often asked, "How does one set up the type of spiritual mentoring you talk about? Do you have a manual, a workbook, or a DVD entitled the Transforming Together series? How do we get it started? And, more importantly, how do we know the results of this type of mentoring, especially if it's done outside the walls of our church building?"

The bottom-line answer is that we don't. We don't know the results, if we're equating results with a body count. That's in better hands than ours. The Godhead knows the results. The Godhead is aware. And I think that is the way the Godhead wants it to be.

However, knowing that this answer may not be well received by everyone reading this book, I did take the liberty of sending out a survey to the incredible *real* women whom I have the extreme privilege of coming alongside of as their mentor. Twelve of them received the survey, and eleven replied. The following is the result of that survey of women ranging in age from midtwenties to sixty.

Question 1:

We all know that there are many options out there for mentoring. Why did you approach me, in particular, to mentor you, considering you had many other options?

"I approached you with a need for a onetime meeting to discuss a marriage issue. The Spirit led me to ask you to mentor me during that meeting. I was attracted to your gracefulness and quietness, to the wisdom of the Word working in your life, and to your wisdom of when to be quiet and when to speak. I was attracted to the way you spoke to me. You made me feel safe; you were someone I could trust. You never criticized me or told me what to do."

"The reason I approached you for mentoring was actually a first impression response. I saw Jesus in you from the moment I met you. I felt our personalities click and I knew the Holy Spirit was going to use you to help me not only grow in Christ but help me with the many issues of this world. I responded to the Holy Spirit's prompting by asking you to be my mentor. After our week of prayer you were very willing to accept, and I'm so glad you did."

"Quite frankly, I had looked for a mentor for many years and was never able to find anyone. The church I attended for a long time was small and full of young Christians. I was discipled briefly through a type of new-Christian training, even though I was not a new Christian at the time, but that was for a scheduled amount of time and went through a specific program. It was a good program, but when our scheduled time was up, that was it. At some point, I began to realize that I was actually one of the more mature Christians at my church and should be mentoring the younger women, as the Bible teaches, but I really had no idea how to go about it. However, I did continue to disciple others using the same new-Christian training program. I had actually given up on ever having a mentor myself, so at the time that I approached you, mentorship wasn't on my radar at all. I was simply in terrible pain and crying out for help to anyone who would listen. You and Don were my Bible study leaders, and so I believe I sent an email to Don and he passed it on to you. Interestingly, I had cried out for help to my entire pastoral church staff and none of them referred me to anyone or offered help of any kind. I thank God that you were there when you were."

"I was having problems dealing with family members. I was not feeling passionate about my walk with Jesus and thought that you might be able to help in those areas."

"I saw Jesus in you. You were sincerely interested in what I had to say. You responded with empathy and wanted to help me see things through Jesus' eyes; how He would handle or look at the situation. I knew I could trust you. You are caring and really interested in people. You are supersensitive to others. You have proved to be fair. You take the time to listen and make the other person feel special. You know how to tie any situation into Jesus' teachings. You have a working understanding of God's Word. You are like a magnet."

"Another friend shared with me that she meets with you as her mentor. She told me how God works on her heart as a result of your times together. So much was going on in my life and God was stirring something in me. I knew I needed some help. I needed to talk to someone, especially about my personal growth. I wanted to be a better, godly mom because I carry so much baggage with me. I've been to a counselor but needed someone in my life in a consistent way, offering spiritual insights and help. The opportunity presented itself at MOPS when you happened to sit at the same table where I was. The topic was speaking to me that day and even the questions we were answering around the table were nudging me to ask for help. After hearing a couple of your talks and knowing that you are a counselor as well as a mentor, I believe the Spirit led me to ask you for help."

"I truly believe it was something that just happened. It was the right time in my life and the right moment in the life of my husband and family. I felt instantly connected to you. I hadn't opened up to another woman before in my life. There was no one I could turn to that wouldn't be judgmental or biased. I had struggled so long with all of my own personal feelings. I desperately needed someone to share them with instead of, through tears, washing them down the shower drain as I had been doing for too long. You were the answer to my prayers."

"I felt safe with you, meaning I knew you weren't going to be judgmental and that you would accept me unconditionally. In addition, I also knew that you love the Lord and I saw great wisdom in you. Essentially, I see you as a wonderful 'Jesus' model."

"I approached you basically because I saw such a difference in my mom's life! It was weird, looking at my mom as a woman and not just my mom! She just started to change; she was more approachable, happier, and calmer. I wanted whatever it was that she had discovered."

"I had a great desire to grow more spiritually, personally, and as a leader, but didn't know exactly how to do that. I was also very grateful that you suggested that we pray about meeting together because I was scared to ask you! I knew that you were the woman whom God wanted me to grow with, but I just didn't know where to begin! Not only was this new territory for me, but it was a new level of accountability that I was not sure I was ready for or wanted."

Do you hear the anticipation, the hunger, the desire, and the relief that they found someone to be in their lives? *You* can be that person for another.

Question 2:

How long have we been meeting?

"One year, but it feels like ten! (That's a good thing!)"

"We've been meeting for three and a half years."

"I'm not sure . . . about three or four years?"

"Fourteen months."

"Has it been four years? You've been walking beside me for four years? You've really been hanging in there, Ele! How did you ever do it?"

"Only three times. Not too long yet!"

"One year, two months . . . and counting."

"We've been meeting for about one year."

"Since January 2008."

"We have been meeting almost two years."

See the variety . . . the longevity? Every six months I do an evaluation with the mentee. That is the time when either one of us is able to say, "Thanks, and so long," or we're able to recommit for another six months. This gives both mentor and mentee the "guilt-free" card to end the mentoring relationship or the opportunity to joyfully continue!

Question 3:

What is your decade in life? Tell me a bit about your family and career.

"I am in my late thirties, have been married for nearly three years, and have two small children. I am a professional educator."

"I am a single professional woman in my early thirties. I have no children."

"I am in my midthirties and have been married almost eleven years. My husband and I have two young children. We have moved quite a bit in those eleven years and I am pleased that we have settled down here in Phoenix."

"I am in my late thirties. This is a first marriage for me and a second one for my husband. Together we have two young children. I am a stay-at-home mom."

"I am in my early forties. My husband and I have three children, ranging in age from eight to fifteen. I have a business out of my home."

"I am in my early thirties and have twins. My husband is a pilot and I am a former kindergarten teacher. I am deeply involved in MOPS."

"I am in my late forties. I have married as well as single adult children. My husband and I have been married for thirty years. I am back in college again!"

"I am in my late fifties. My children are grown and out of the home. I am a professional businesswoman."

"I am in my early sixties. I can't believe that! I am a wife, mother, grandmother, and a professional woman."

You can see from these answers that age doesn't matter and stage of life doesn't matter. Heart attitude is what matters.

Question 4:

To your knowledge, how many lives is the Spirit intentionally influencing for Himself through you as a result of your being mentored?

"Three in particular: my mom, my husband, and a teenager that I mentor."

"Twenty for sure."

"Four directly. Also sixteen more that I work with almost daily."

"I'd say at least twenty, and seven more intimate relationships as well."

"I am a light to my family, my friends, the children I teach in Sunday school weekly, and the women at my table in MOPS. I'd say a lot more than I realized before thinking through this question! Perhaps around twenty-five."

"The Spirit is influencing, through me, more people than I really realize. There is a ripple effect that seems to reach out beyond my knowledge and every little word or action makes a difference! My relationship with my husband has become stronger, more honest, and passionate. We seek God's Word first, and through the mentor meetings I have with you, I feel supported and guided in the right direction. My mom and my brother are seeing the joy that I once experienced with Jesus come back. My conversations with them have changed for the better. One of my closest girlfriends has started coming to church with me and recently gave her life to Christ! My kids have started asking questions about what it means to have 'Jesus in their hearts.' I celebrate every time the subject comes up. As a MOPS leader, I influence seventy-five plus women whether I realize it or not. The way I live, the words that I speak, and the smallest action, whether positive or negative, all play a part in what influence I provide. I live for the Lord! Right now I would say that the Spirit is directly influencing about ninety-six people through my life. Praise His name!"

"A minimum of ten close family members and five at work."

"So far two, with the hope of more."

"Five immediate family members, six friends, five neighbors, and two close friends. That makes eighteen people! Wow, I had no idea!"

"This will remain to be seen either later in this life or in the next. I am sure I have an influence on many people." (I know the influence God has given this woman on the lives of others. Conservatively speaking I would say at least fifty lives are influenced regularly by the Spirit through her.)

All added up, that makes a whopping 276 people who are being directly influenced by the Holy Spirit through *eleven* lives! For those really into numerical results, that means that the growth percentile is 2,500 percent . . . all accomplished by living life-on-life, opening the living Word of God, and growing together in Him! There is no program, no building, no budget, no books, just following Jesus' example by coming alongside of another in her journey, partnering with who the Holy Spirit is being in her life, infusing truth into her reality, and then stepping back and giving God the glory for who He is in the life of that other person. Keep in mind, the vast majority of those whom the Spirit influences through these women are not people who go to church. That 2,500 percent is basically made up of people outside of normal church influence! That means these are not the same people over and over who hear, who attend, and who already have opportunity to grow. The Spirit is not hindered. In fact, the Spirit of God delights in meeting people "who" they are and moving them to "who" they need to be in Him!

Question 5:

Please comment on our usual meeting place of Starbucks. Is this comfortable for you?

"Meeting at Starbucks is fine with me!"

"I love the coffee places!"

"Meeting at Starbucks is fine. Sometimes I feel it's a little too open, but not usually. (Just my insecurity!)"

"I like that it's not at my house because I am not focusing on what I need to do at home or if the floor is a mess! The 'buzz' of people constantly going in and out actually allows me to focus, and I like that. It also allows for the ripple effect to occur. You never know who is listening or watching and who we can make an impact on!"

"We meet at my house. I thank God for your generosity and flexibility! This works great for me and my kids! They are usually either napping or having 'quiet time' in their room."

"I love meeting at Starbucks as it's a treat when one is a mother of little ones. I love being there with you. Sometimes we meet at home and that's fun, too, because I like you getting to be in my home, where so much of life happens!"

"I love where we meet . . . the feeling of that place feels right. The people are great there."

"Starbucks is fine. It's pretty laid back and it's a change of scenery for me. The weather here in Phoenix is perfect for outdoor meetings. The only thing that is annoying at times is when a noisy car parks next to us, but I manage to filter that out."

"At times I feel Starbucks is a bit too open, but I don't have a better alternative. I wonder if the 'openness' discourages the type of deep, powerful, and passionate prayer that sometimes needs to take place. I don't remember us praying together for a very long time. I know you pray for me, but I miss you praying *with* me."

"It's fine for me."

It seems as if the surroundings are important to these women. Obviously, you don't *have* to be at Starbucks to have a spiritually effective mentoring session. And please don't throw out the *concept* of spiritual mentoring because you don't happen to like Starbucks, or if you live in a place where there are no cozy coffee shops. Pick your own special place. Ask your mentee what would work best for her. The point is to be flexible. Effective mentoring can occur wherever two people want to meet with Jesus.

Question 6:

Would you be willing to share any specific examples of how our time together has encouraged or helped you?

"Some of the issues I have looked at in a new way on a personal level would be my responsibilities as a parent, my feelings in regard to personal guilt, a new understanding of how others see me, and my own look at 'Who am I?'"

"I remember a specific time when my husband and I had to confront our son and his girlfriend on some very serious issues. Fortunately, the girlfriend's parents were in complete agreement with us and the four of us were able to present a united front to our children. Ele worked with me, and together we planned details such as where to meet, what to say, and how to say it in a way that would be received. When I shared the tentative plan with the other parents, they were so blessed, and they expressed the relief they felt at having a guide to keep us focused in a potentially volatile situation. The meeting went incredibly well and eventually our son was able to understand just how unhealthy the relationship really was. A short while later, you and your husband were able to experience the transformation in our son's life as you watched him play the guitar at a worship service. You said you couldn't take your eyes off of him; that he looked like someone who had been set free. Indeed he was."

"I am so blessed that you are investing in me. I won't forget how you explained to me what *blessing* means—a dimensional approval. That's how I feel each time we meet. Now I'm trying to apply that to those whom I love, beginning with my husband and son. The other thing is from John 1:14, where it says that Jesus is 'full of grace and truth.' Grace comes first, and then truth enters. I won't forget your encouragement to me about taking things in with grace first, and then applying truth. You said something like grace is the forerunner that prepares the way for truth. This is something I struggle with and I'm really trying to work on."

"The most important thing that comes to mind is my relationship with my children. It's still not where I want it to be nor where Christ would have it be. You've helped clarify how truth, application, sensitivity, forgiveness, understanding, and prayer are *tools* to be used. I've also learned that it's important to ask the right questions at the right time. I'm still working on it. I mess up sometimes but I pray that my children will know Him soon. I know that our relationship is part of that process."

"I was going home for the holiday to an extremely large Italian family. I knew I would have to deal with tons of old habits, arguing, verbal explosions, and trying to please too much . . . with Italian matriarchs! But just as God would have it, He had you and me study John 3:21 right before my trip. The advice received in that verse turned what could have been a tense visit into a wonderful time! We talked about how living by the truth enables a person to come into the light. Light either reveals truth or exposes an area of need in a life. So, when my cousin came to me to cry on my shoulder as she always does, I invited her to sit in a private corner with me. I let her share and then, at the right moment, I 'infused truth into her reality'! The light came on in her eyes and it was a wonderfully positive outcome!"

"You have been a living example to me of how the Word of God can work in a person's life. Anytime I have a conflict, a concern, or a question about something or someone in my life, you almost always dive *directly into the Bible!* You don't just give me your opinion! I notice that every time, and I praise God for that example."

"The one that jumps out at me happened just recently. I was sharing with you about where God was taking me with stepping into a mentoring role with three ladies. At that time I did not consider myself a mentor—rather a leader—and you put it right out there that I was a mentor! Without the time that we had spent together, I would not have anything to model my new role after, and for that I am truly grateful."

"Our times together have helped me have a desire to better myself in the area of communication. It has made me a more compassionate person, with a desire to be more encouraging and uplifting in my relationships."

"I am convinced that you made me look at my marriage in a different way. I know through you that this time we have on earth is but a speck and I must try to make the most of this time. I have a better relationship with my husband because of your advice and the emphasis you have placed on *growing stronger in Christ.* You have great communication skills. You ask great questions, and you are empathetic. I have learned how to relate better with people from your example. You often have a game or activity to accomplish the goal of getting to know someone better and getting one to open up and help people verbalize."

"I feel motivated to read God's Word each time we meet! I have felt encouraged with my marriage. I have seen overall improvement with our communication and affection for each other."

Encouragement comes where the need is the greatest. Personal issues were dealt with. Family stresses were attended to. Scriptural insights were shared, and spiritual truths were infused. A marriage was saved. A mentee was challenged to become a mentor to others in her life! This is encouragement in "work clothes," through everyday life. You can be the one to offer that to another.

Question 7:

We usually meet for around two hours. Others I have talked to just can't believe that we spend that much time together without a study guide! Please comment on the format of the time together. Is it helpful? Is it too slow? Does it work for you?

"I love the format of our time together because that allows the Holy Spirit to direct our time. In addition, our time feels complete to me, meaning I don't feel there is any unfinished business."

"Yes, two hours is average. I like everything about our meeting and wouldn't change anything."

"Our time together is perfect. If anything, it's too short!"

"I love that the two hours goes where God takes us. We usually start with a check-in time on how things are going and what has been happening with both of us and finish with time in the Bible. Through our conversation, we usually find ourselves looking up and reading several Scriptures that apply to the top- ics at hand. Outside of our meeting time, I have a hard time fol- lowing a study guide now, quite honestly! I feel that they keep my learning confined to a 'box,' and I have a hard time not straying once my mind focuses on that. When I am able to slow down and allow the Holy Spirit to ask the questions and be my study Guide, I grasp and learn what's appropriate for me at that moment. When I go back to a Scripture that I have already read, I almost always find something new that I can grow from. It's all about what He has for us in the Scripture at that moment in time."

"This type of scenario allows the Lord to work in our meeting, our conversation, and our results. Thank you for being such a great example. I thank God for softening your heart and giving you a heart and mind that is so eager to seek His truth."

"I always leave our time together, asking, 'Where did the time go?' as I skip off with a smile and join my loved ones. Our time together is so full of God's truth in life experiences, questions, more questions, thoughts, sharing, direction, giggles, and oc- casionally a few tears. Mostly I end up feeling like we're a team as we huddle, get encouragement from the Godhead, and hear, 'Go team!'"

"I know that the Spirit will take us wherever we need to go. It's no surprise anymore when what we are going to study is *ex- actly* what I needed to hear for my family or work situation."
"There's a lot of deep stuff that we cover. I look forward to our meetings and wouldn't change the format at all. Covering

Scripture and answering the questions that arise from them is plenty. It's very deep and meaningful to me. I'm finding that it's helpful for me to review my notes of what we covered after the meeting to try to keep it in my mind. The time we spend together flies by fast!"

"The first thirty to forty-five minutes is usually catching up with personal issues, family, etc. Although there is not a study guide, you have given questions from the Scripture text to be answered. You have encouraged me to come up with my own questions as well. Given all that, two hours is just about right."

People need the gift of time. We see time and time again in the Gospels that Jesus lingered, stayed awhile, remained, or delayed in order to spend time with people. He knew the importance of the gift of time. Can we offer anything less?

Question 8:

How is the Spirit growing you through this mentoring relationship?

"This is ever-changing. I think I have had some 'lightbulb' moments that have helped me with new ways to look at issues in life. When I am diligent in my studies, life is smoother and more tolerable. When things get tough, I go to my knees sooner and quicker. Having a mentoring relationship provides accountability, which was not always present in the past."

"I can't imagine my life without being around someone who searches always for truth in our daily lives. Having you help me understand the teachings of the Word of God and challenge me (without judging me) on how to apply these in my life has been so helpful and so freeing. I will never be the same and I feel sorry for people who don't know what truth is; I now realize that that is what life is about—passing truth on. I try to do that as well."

"You have taught me to live my life according to the way Jesus would. This truth is to love Jesus and to love people. You have taught me to live by the Bible and follow the ways of the Word, not wavering from that. You have made real the reason I am here: to love Jesus, to love others, and to serve as He served. Through your example and teaching, I have learned how to do these things. The sharing of truth through the Word of God that you provide is real and applicable. You have helped me grow in faith and relationships in a way I could have never done on my own. I have grown in the past three years more than any other time."

"So far the Holy Spirit is challenging me to look into and at myself from my own perspective and from God's perspective—trying to understand who I am, and especially who I should be in Christ."

"The Spirit is teaching me to love. I am learning to die to myself. God is using my husband and children in this process."

"Ele, you're a beautiful, active example of seeking the Spirit, listening to the Spirit, and allowing the Spirit to work in every situation. When I try to emulate this, it brings peace and God's wisdom to my marriage, to my parenting, and to my sisters in Jesus."

"As our mentoring relationship progresses, I believe that the greatest growth has been in hearing the Spirit in me and moving on it. I love seeing how Jesus 'lived it' and then listening as the Spirit directs me to live it as well! Throughout our times together, I often have had no idea what would be revealed to me. But as a result of hearing the Spirit's voice with clarity, I'd say that my relationships on all levels have grown. Having a mentor to walk alongside of me, to listen, to encourage, to point out things, and to exhort me once in a while has added vibrancy to my inner person. You affirm me as a daughter, a sister, a wife, a friend, a mother, and a person in Christ Jesus."

"Through this relationship I have seen more growth than I would have ever imagined. I have been able to open up in confidence and share issues and concerns knowing that the response will be appropriate and honest. My relationship with Jesus has become stronger daily, and I am more in tune with *His* path, not mine. I feel a sense of security now. My daily stress as a mom, a leader, a woman, and just in general has greatly decreased because I know that the burden is not mine to carry alone. I have had the opportunity to see my personal growth as a leader and have come to recognize the spiritual gift that I have been blessed with. During our meetings I have been able to express concerns and praises regarding leadership and am able to know that the advice that I seek comes through my mentor from God because it is always based on biblical principles. One of the greatest struggles that I face as a Christian is being in the Bible and knowing exactly how to 'dig in' and take something from what I read by myself and for myself. I had always read to just 'get through it' but I truly was not taking much from it! These mentor meetings have taught me how to do that and what I have gained through asking myself the questions that are posed in the text and taking it a small chunk at a time is priceless. I am now in the Word daily and am thirsty for more!"

Do you hear the emphasis? It's on Jesus! It's on living the way Jesus would live. It's on listening for and hearing the voice of the Holy Spirit through the reading of God's Word. It's on being hungry and thirsty for more of God, more truth. May that always be where the emphasis is!

Question 9:

Is there anything else you would like to share?

> "Thank you, from the bottom of my heart, for all that you have invested in my life, my family, and those around you. God has worked through you, and because of your faithfulness, many blessings will come. I look forward to a forever friendship. I love you, Ele!"

> "I am blessed by the time you spend with me, Ele. May God bless you and use this book to bless others in a way that grows them closer to Jesus with a great big smile on their face! May they have a shining compass with Jesus through their lives with their own mentors. Thank You, Lord!"

> "Ele, you are the mother, sister, and friend that I never had. I hungered for that and desire to 'be' for another as well! You are a beautiful, fallible woman whom God has graced with His wisdom from heaven. I truly believe that. Thank you for giving your heart, soul, and mind to Jesus and, in turn, to my husband, family, and friends. Ultimately the glory goes to God! I pray for you often as a leader, a teacher, and a Christ-follower. I pray for His will to be done in your life, for God's protection for you and Don. I pray for continued courage, perseverance, and wisdom. I love you! Thank you!"

> "Thank you so much for meeting with me. I am truly enjoying the journey!"

"Thank you for investing in me. I am being blessed! I thank God for you!"

"I just want to say that I love you and I'm so glad you are in my life!"

"Thank you for not judging me when I have chosen to live in a way other than how I know I should be living. At times it's just too hard to make the right choice. I am growing, and I thank God that you accept me just as I am. I need someone to be Jesus in my life. You're the one."

"Every time you confirm that we're going to get together, I ask the question, 'Why me?' Then I say, 'Why not me? This has to be God's doing!' God loves *me* too! I have tears in my eyes now while I'm typing this to you. Please just keep hanging in there with me. I'm trying to 'get there.' You have made a major mark on my life. I get it, Ele. I know what you're up to! It only takes *one* believer to affect a few, then more, and then *those* believers affect more and it just keeps multiplying. That's God's plan."

Focus on relationships. Leave the results to God!

Afterword

So how was the read? Was it encouraging? Helpful? Insightful? Frustrating? Irritating? However you feel about it, I want you to leave this book with some thoughts to consider.

If what has been shared in these pages resonates with your spirit, your will, your mind, and your emotions, then my encouragement to you would be to pray and ask God to grant you the desire of your heart—to mentor or to be mentored in the way presented to you in this book. Go back and reread the book with pen in hand, and underline everything that the Spirit highlights for you. Make those concepts and those ideas your prayer to see how God wants to use them in your life. If you have a mentoring program in your church, don't disturb it. Let the Spirit continue there. Believe me, there are *plenty* of Christ-followers who are also looking for another type of mentoring. Pray. Ask Jesus to guide you, to teach you, and to lead you to that person whom you would like to mentor you. Or if you are qualified to be a mentor, ask the Spirit to lead someone to you to be mentored.

If you are disgruntled by what has been shared in these pages, then I would encourage you to pray as well. Pray for insight to glean *something* helpful! Pray for me, that I would remain steadfast in Jesus, my

Rock and my Salvation. Write to me and interact with me if you would like to do so. What I would ask of you as well is to not take "potshots" at what is presented in these pages. The concepts shared here are effective. They draw people to Jesus and infuse truth into their reality as they grow in Him. They are not bad ideas. They may not be *your* ideas, and that's fine. Just don't give any more ammunition to the mutual enemy of our souls. We do that enough already as followers of Jesus, don't we?

The point is that I encourage you to respond to this book in some way. Interact with it! Don't just read it and say, "Oh, how sweet!" As followers of Jesus, we should be miles from that sort of unproductive sentiment. If you're not either a mentor or a mentee, pray and ask God to give you direction, guidance, and someone else in your life with whom to begin purposefully growing. Your life will never be the same as a result!

I want to leave you with a very specific verse about the subject of mentoring." [Timothy], my son, be strong in the grace that is in Christ Jesus. And the things you have heard me say in the presence of many witnesses entrust to reliable men who will also be qualified to teach others" (2 Timothy 2:1–2). By now I know you see it. But allow me to boil it down for you in order that the intent of these verses will be crystal clear: "Take what you know and give it to someone else." That's it. "Take what you know ('And the things you have heard me say in the presence of many witnesses') and give it to someone else ('entrust to reliable [people] who will also be qualified to teach others')."

That's it in a nutshell. Take what you know about Jesus and pass it on to someone else. Jesus was our example. The Holy Spirit is our Teacher. The Godhead is glorified through us as followers of Jesus. Come alongside of another, partner with the Holy Spirit in who He is being in her life, and infuse truth into her reality. Take what you know about Jesus and pass it on.

Do you hear the beat? Do you see the succession? It goes from many witnesses who knew Jesus while He was here on earth, to those before us, to us, to those around us, to those who are to come. You are invited to join in on the succession that began when Jesus walked this earth: mentor and be mentored. You will never turn back.

My prayer for you is that the Holy Spirit will infuse His truth into your reality as you purpose to come alongside of another, partner with the Holy Spirit in that life, and infuse truth into that person's reality. That succession invites you to join with millions of others who are discovering the incredible depth of life that comes from transforming together in Him.

WOMEN MENTORING WOMEN

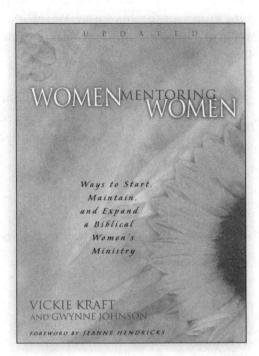

ISBN-13: 978-0-8024-4889-7

UPDATED

WOMEN MENTORING WOMEN

Ways to Start,
Maintain,
and Expand
a Biblical
Women's
Ministry

VICKIE KRAFT
AND GWYNNE JOHNSON

FOREWORD BY JEANNE HENDRICKS

The 21st Century has brought a new urgency for Christian women to search for meaningful relationships where they can live out their faith. This is due in part to our increasingly secular lifestyle and the radical changes in marriage and family life that have isolated and discouraged many women. *Women Mentoring Women* offers the solution to a chronic weakness in churches: the lack of involvement of wives, sisters, mothers, and daughters in vital women's ministries.

MOODY
PUBLISHERS.

1-800-678-8812 · MOODYPUBLISHERS.COM

SHEPHERDING A WOMAN'S HEART

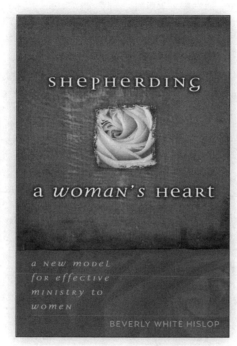

Women in pain populate every congregation. Left to themselves, many will become discouraged and leave the church. But pastors cannot adequately care for the needs of everyone. Beverly White Hislop has written *Shepherding a Woman's Heart* to challenge pastors to infuse to women in their churches with the same spirit that moves them to care for their flock. This amazing resource provides substantial guidance on how to properly equip healthy women to come forward and nurture hurting women.

1-800-678-8812 · MOODYPUBLISHERS.COM

LEADING WOMEN WHO WOUND

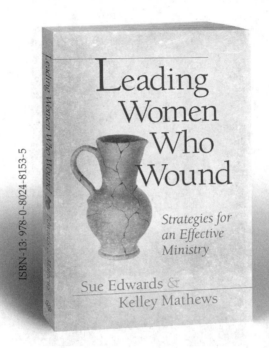

Leading Women Who Wound shows women how to effectively deal with conflict
within their ministries. Seasoned women's ministry leaders themselves,
Sue Edwards and Kelley Mathews walk through several different aspects of conflict
resolution including self examination, identification of potential sources of conflict,
tools for conflict resolution, and insight on how to prevent and move beyond conflict
to minister to those who have been sources of contention.

MOODY
PUBLISHERS.

1-800-678-8812 · MOODYPUBLISHERS.COM

TRANSFORMING FOR A PURPOSE

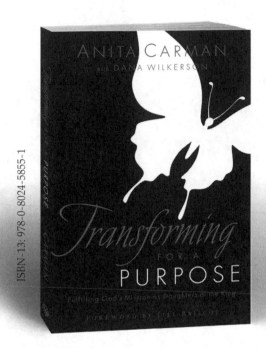

Women in ministry face needs that are often overlooked by the local
church and consequently remain underdeveloped as they seek
to lead and guide those in their care.

Anita Carman walks you through the need to shape emotions that will
guard and fulfill God's purpose, and the need to bond in order to build a
community of authentic lasting friendships.

MOODY
PUBLISHERS.

1-800-678-8812 · MOODYPUBLISHERS.COM